Published by Nona Books in 2023

First edition; First printing

Illustrations and design © 2023 Nona Books

Printed in the United States of America

www.nonakid.com

Copyright © 2023
By Nona Books

BIRD WATCHING JOURNAL

The Ultimate Birding Journal for Young Explorers

Nona Books

this journal belongs to:

from the author

Dear young bird enthusiasts,

First of all, I would like to say how thrilled I am that you have decided to keep a bird journal! Observing and recording the birds around us is a fantastic way to learn more about the natural world and to appreciate the beauty of these feathered creatures.

As the author of this journal, I wanted to share a few thoughts with you. Remember, the journal is your personal space to record your observations, thoughts, and feelings. There is no right or wrong way to keep a journal. Feel free to be creative and make it your own.

Also, don't be discouraged if you don't see many birds at first. It can take time and patience to spot them. The more you watch, the more you'll notice, and soon you'll start recognizing the different species and their behaviors.

Lastly, I encourage you to continue learning about birds and their habitats. There are so many fascinating facts to discover, and by doing so, you will develop a deeper appreciation for the birds around you.

I hope this journal brings you as much joy and fascination as it has brought me.

Happy bird watching!

Yours,
Iris.

Table of Contents

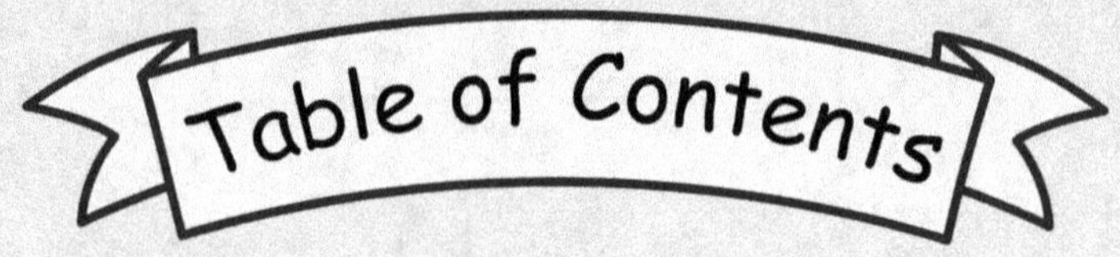

PART 1 – BIRD WATCHING LOGS

PART 2 – BIRD FUN

PART 3 – BIRD IDENTIFICATION

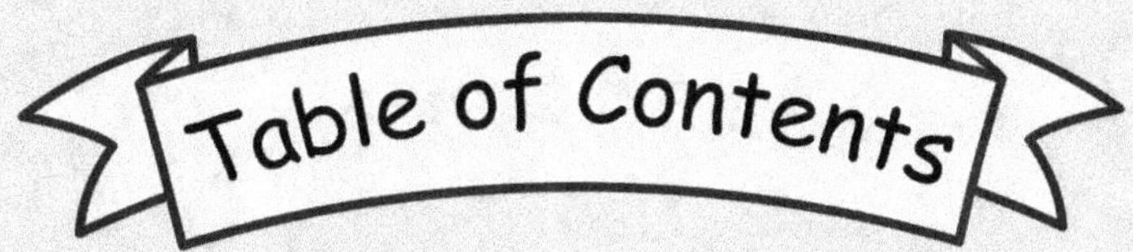

Table of Contents

PART 3 - BIRD IDENTIFICATION (cont.)

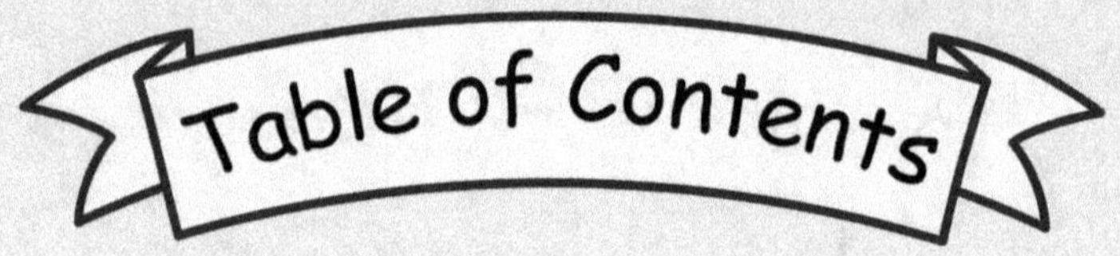

Table of Contents

PART 3 – BIRD IDENTIFICATION (cont.)

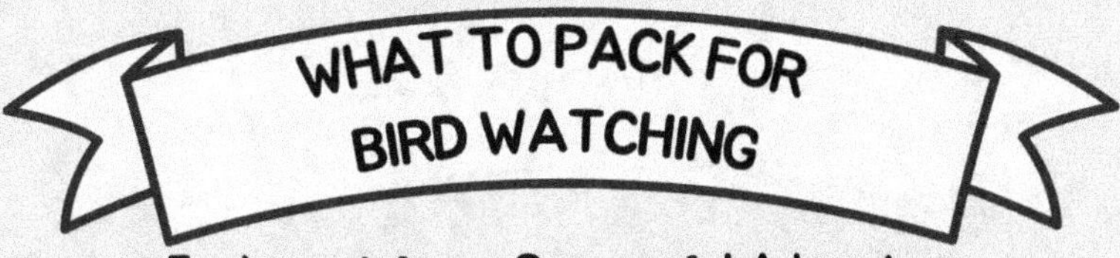

WHAT TO PACK FOR BIRD WATCHING

Equipment for a Successful Adventure

Are you ready for an exciting birdwatching adventure? Here is a list of the essential equipment you'll need to have the best time on your birdwatching trip!

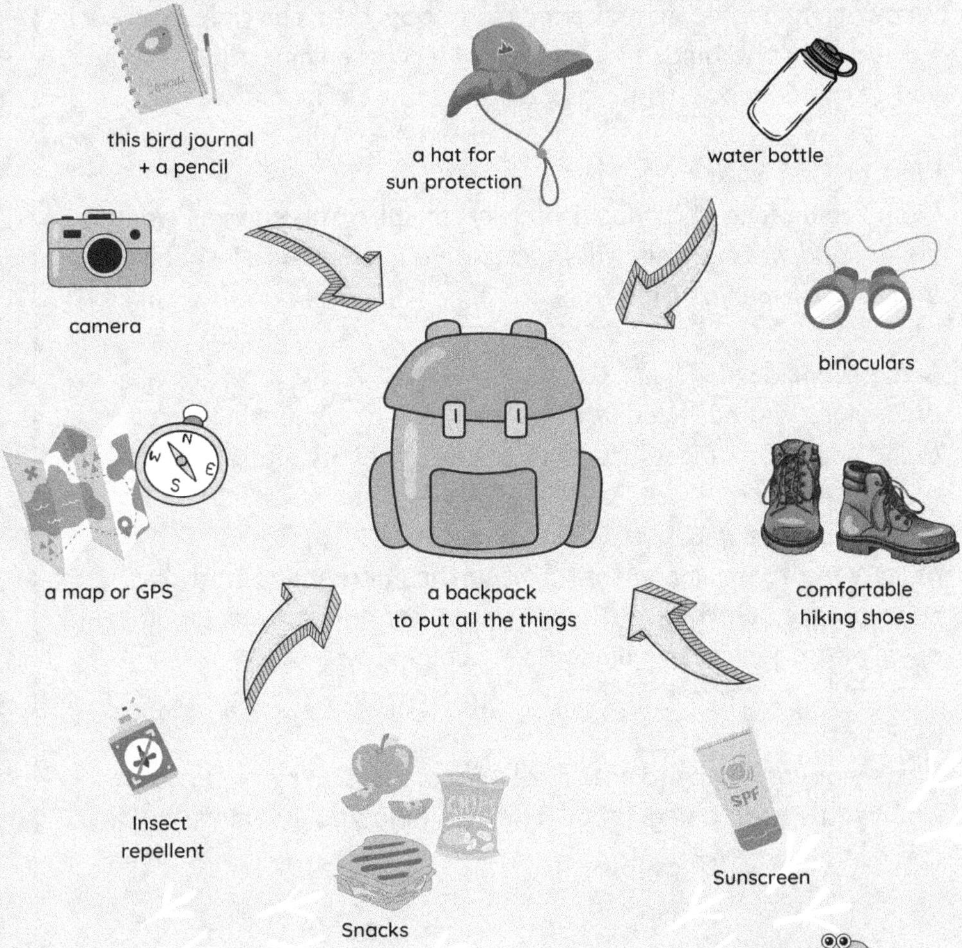

this bird journal + a pencil
a hat for sun protection
water bottle
camera
binoculars
a map or GPS
a backpack to put all the things
comfortable hiking shoes
Insect repellent
Snacks
Sunscreen

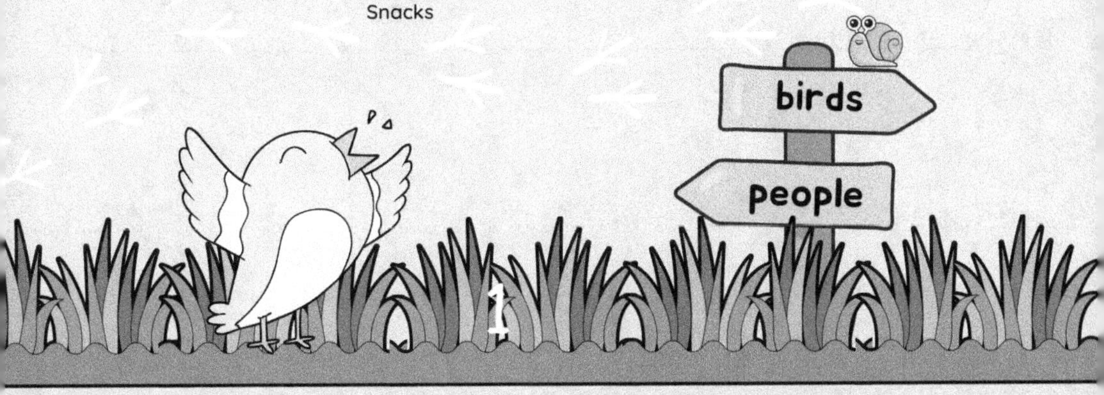

birds
people

Birdwatching is a fun and exciting hobby that can help you learn more about the birds in your area. Here are some tips to help you get the most out of your birdwatching experience:

Find a good spot
Look for a place that has a variety of habitats, such as woods, fields, and water. This will increase your chances of seeing different types of birds.

Bring binoculars
Binoculars will help you get a closer look at birds that are far away. Look for binoculars that are lightweight and easy to carry.

Dress for the weather
Make sure to wear comfortable clothes and shoes that are appropriate for the weather. Bring a hat and sunscreen on sunny days, and a jacket or raincoat on cooler days.

Be quiet
Birds are easily frightened by loud noises, so try to be quiet when you're watching them. This will help you see more birds and get closer to them.

Be patient
Birdwatching requires patience, as birds can be elusive and hard
to spot. Take your time and enjoy the scenery while you wait for
birds to appear.

Learn bird calls
Many birds have distinct calls that can help you identify them.
Listen for bird calls and try to match them to the birds you see.

Respect nature
Remember to respect the birds and their habitats. Do not
disturb nests or interfere with birds in any way. Leave the area
as you found it, and do not litter.

By following these tips, you can have a great birdwatching
experience and learn more about the birds in your area.

Happy birdwatching!

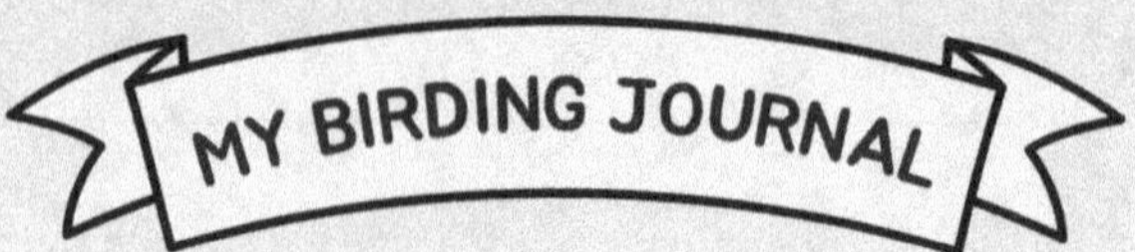

DATE:

SEASON:

WEATHER:

TIME:

HABITAT:

TEMPERATURE:

LOCATION:

BIRD'S NAME:	NESTING:
COLOR AND MARKINGS:	BIRD'S BEHAVIOR:
MALE/FEMALE/NOT SURE	NUMBER OF BIRDS OBSERVED:

BIRD LOCATION

ground ☐

tree ☐

air ☐

bush ☐

feeder ☐

other:

NOTES

BIRD'S SKETCH

DATE:

SEASON:

WEATHER:

TIME:

HABITAT:

TEMPERATURE:

LOCATION:

BIRD'S NAME:	NESTING:
COLOR AND MARKINGS:	BIRD'S BEHAVIOR:
MALE/FEMALE/NOT SURE	NUMBER OF BIRDS OBSERVED:

BIRD LOCATION

ground ☐
tree ☐
air ☐
bush ☐
feeder ☐
other:

NOTES

BIRD'S SKETCH

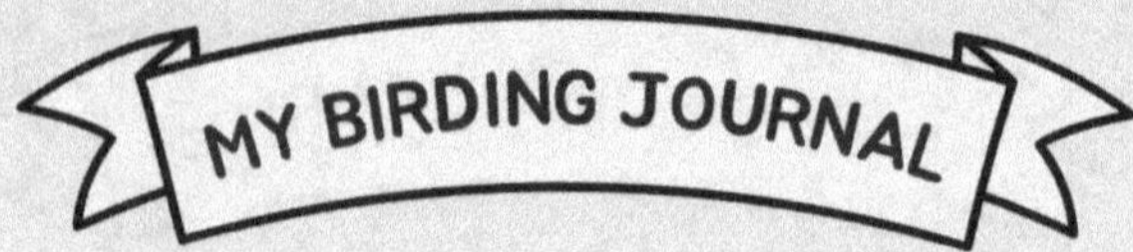

DATE:

SEASON:

WEATHER:

TIME:

HABITAT:

TEMPERATURE:

LOCATION:

BIRD'S NAME:

NESTING:

COLOR AND MARKINGS:

BIRD'S BEHAVIOR:

MALE/FEMALE/NOT SURE

NUMBER OF BIRDS OBSERVED:

BIRD LOCATION

ground ☐

tree ☐

air ☐

bush ☐

feeder ☐

other:

NOTES

BIRD'S SKETCH

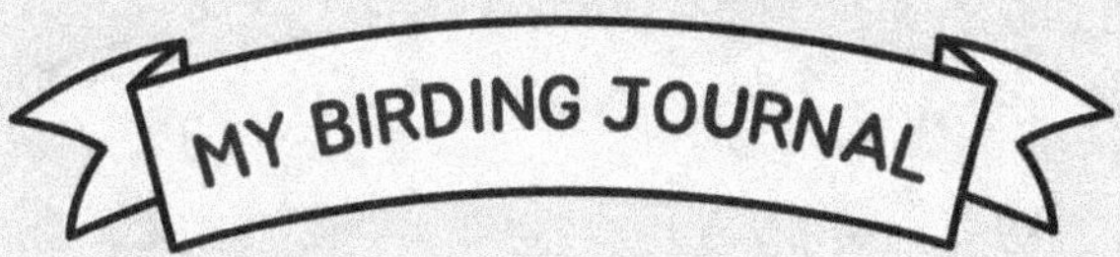

DATE:

SEASON:

WEATHER:

TIME:

HABITAT:

TEMPERATURE:

LOCATION:

BIRD'S NAME:

NESTING:

COLOR AND MARKINGS:

BIRD'S BEHAVIOR:

MALE/FEMALE/NOT SURE

NUMBER OF BIRDS OBSERVED:

BIRD LOCATION

ground ☐
tree ☐
air ☐
bush ☐
feeder ☐
other:

NOTES

BIRD'S SKETCH

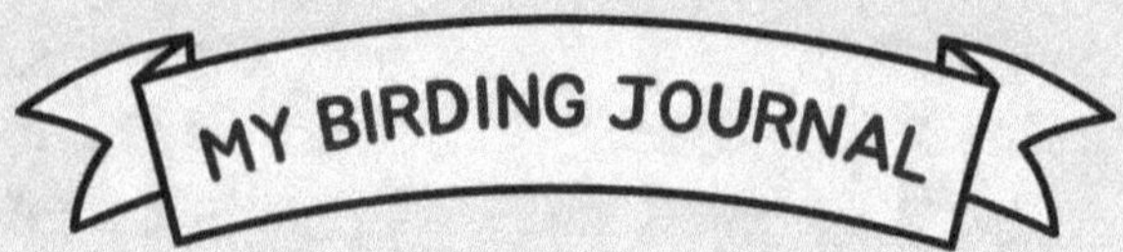

DATE:

SEASON:

WEATHER:

TIME:

HABITAT:

TEMPERATURE:

LOCATION:

BIRD'S NAME:

NESTING:

COLOR AND MARKINGS:

BIRD'S BEHAVIOR:

MALE/FEMALE/NOT SURE

NUMBER OF BIRDS OBSERVED:

BIRD LOCATION

ground ☐
tree ☐
air ☐
bush ☐
feeder ☐
other:

NOTES

BIRD'S SKETCH

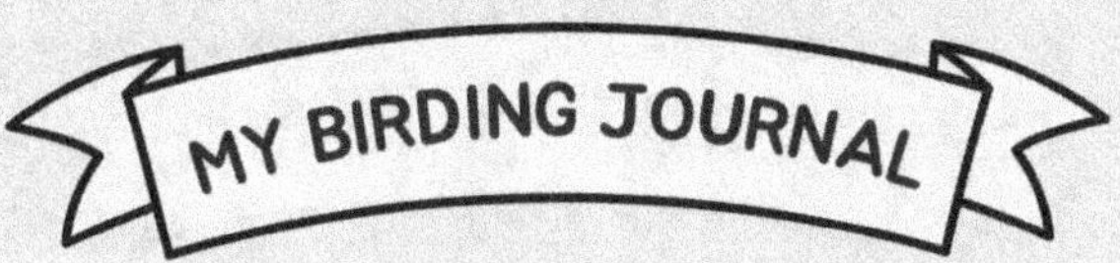

MY BIRDING JOURNAL

DATE:

SEASON:

WEATHER:

TIME:

HABITAT:

TEMPERATURE:

LOCATION:

BIRD'S NAME:

NESTING:

COLOR AND MARKINGS:

BIRD'S BEHAVIOR:

MALE/FEMALE/NOT SURE

NUMBER OF BIRDS OBSERVED:

BIRD LOCATION

ground ☐

tree ☐

air ☐

bush ☐

feeder ☐

other:

NOTES

BIRD'S SKETCH

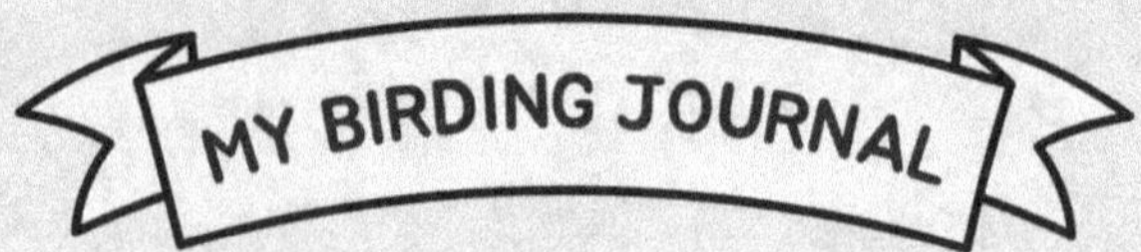

DATE:

SEASON:

WEATHER:

TIME:

HABITAT:

TEMPERATURE:

LOCATION:

BIRD'S NAME:

NESTING:

COLOR AND MARKINGS:

BIRD'S BEHAVIOR:

MALE/FEMALE/NOT SURE

NUMBER OF BIRDS OBSERVED:

BIRD LOCATION

ground ☐
tree ☐
air ☐
bush ☐
feeder ☐
other:

NOTES

BIRD'S SKETCH

DATE:

SEASON:

WEATHER:

TIME:

HABITAT:

TEMPERATURE:

LOCATION:

BIRD'S NAME:	NESTING:
COLOR AND MARKINGS:	BIRD'S BEHAVIOR:
MALE/FEMALE/NOT SURE	NUMBER OF BIRDS OBSERVED:

BIRD LOCATION

ground ☐

tree ☐

air ☐

bush ☐

feeder ☐

other:

NOTES

BIRD'S SKETCH

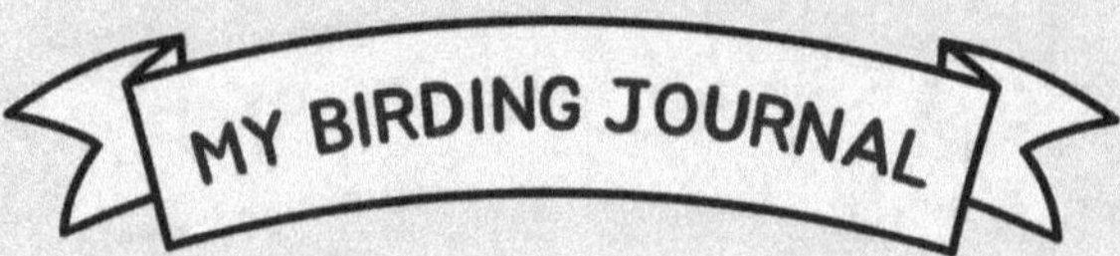

DATE:

SEASON:

WEATHER:

TIME:

HABITAT:

TEMPERATURE:

LOCATION:

BIRD'S NAME:

NESTING:

COLOR AND MARKINGS:

BIRD'S BEHAVIOR:

MALE/FEMALE/NOT SURE

NUMBER OF BIRDS OBSERVED:

BIRD LOCATION

ground

tree

air

bush

feeder

other:

NOTES

BIRD'S SKETCH

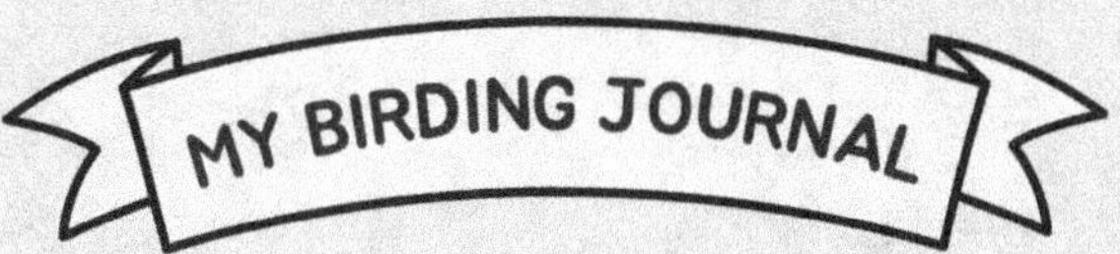

DATE:

SEASON:

WEATHER:

TIME:

HABITAT:

TEMPERATURE:

LOCATION:

BIRD'S NAME:	NESTING:
COLOR AND MARKINGS:	BIRD'S BEHAVIOR:
MALE/FEMALE/NOT SURE	NUMBER OF BIRDS OBSERVED:

BIRD LOCATION

ground ☐

tree ☐

air ☐

bush ☐

feeder ☐

other:

NOTES

BIRD'S SKETCH

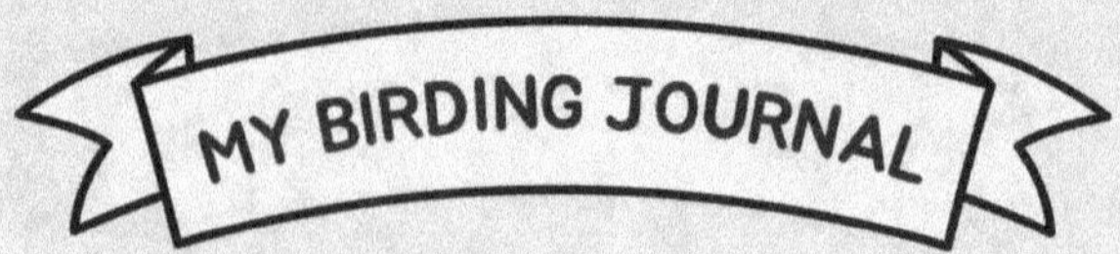

DATE:

SEASON:

WEATHER:

TIME:

HABITAT:

TEMPERATURE:

LOCATION:

BIRD'S NAME:

NESTING:

COLOR AND MARKINGS:

BIRD'S BEHAVIOR:

MALE/FEMALE/NOT SURE

NUMBER OF BIRDS OBSERVED:

BIRD LOCATION

ground ☐

tree ☐

air ☐

bush ☐

feeder ☐

other:

NOTES

BIRD'S SKETCH

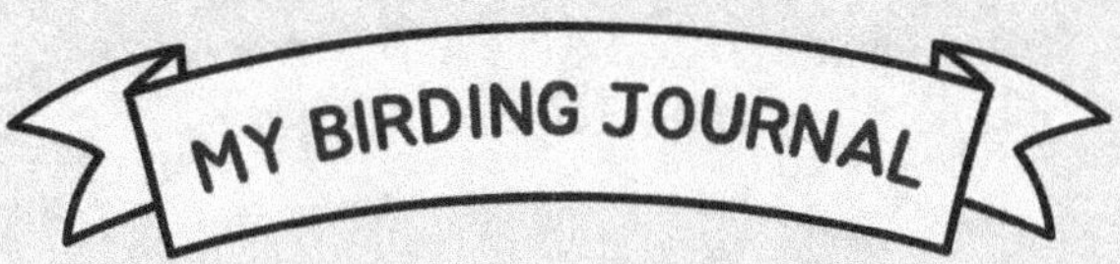

DATE:

SEASON:

WEATHER:

TIME:

HABITAT:

TEMPERATURE:

LOCATION:

BIRD'S NAME:	NESTING:
COLOR AND MARKINGS:	BIRD'S BEHAVIOR:
MALE/FEMALE/NOT SURE	NUMBER OF BIRDS OBSERVED:

BIRD LOCATION

ground

tree

air

bush

feeder

other:

NOTES

BIRD'S SKETCH

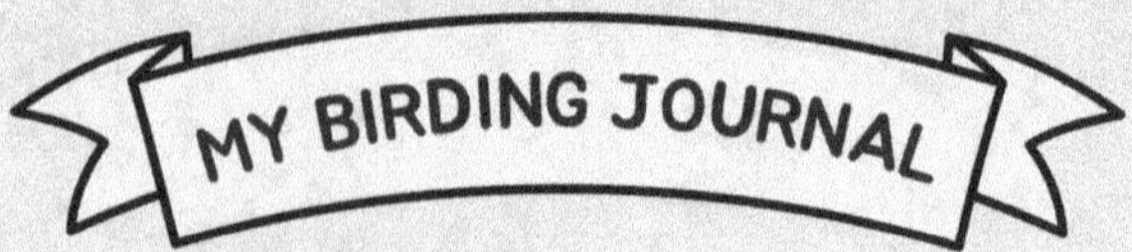

DATE:

SEASON:

WEATHER:

TIME:

HABITAT:

TEMPERATURE:

LOCATION:

BIRD'S NAME:

NESTING:

COLOR AND MARKINGS:

BIRD'S BEHAVIOR:

MALE/FEMALE/NOT SURE

NUMBER OF BIRDS OBSERVED:

BIRD LOCATION

ground ☐

tree ☐

air ☐

bush ☐

feeder ☐

other:

NOTES

BIRD'S SKETCH

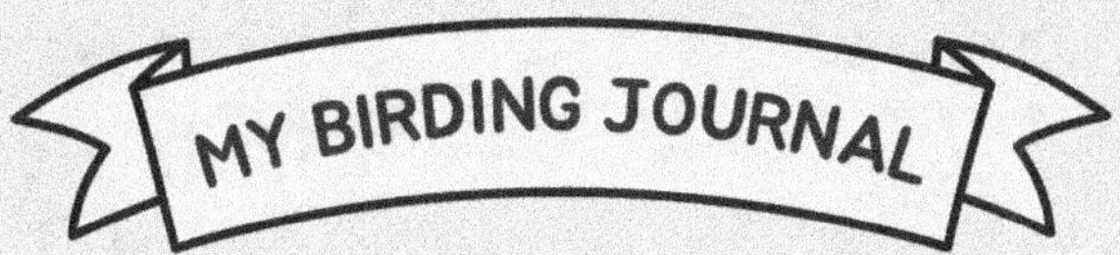

DATE:

SEASON:

WEATHER:

TIME:

HABITAT:

TEMPERATURE:

LOCATION:

BIRD'S NAME:

NESTING:

COLOR AND MARKINGS:

BIRD'S BEHAVIOR:

MALE/FEMALE/NOT SURE

NUMBER OF BIRDS OBSERVED:

BIRD LOCATION

ground ☐

tree ☐

air ☐

bush ☐

feeder ☐

other:

NOTES

BIRD'S SKETCH

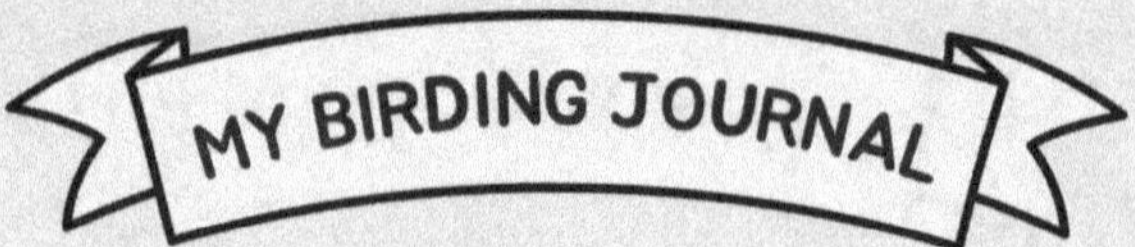

DATE:

SEASON:

WEATHER:

TIME:

HABITAT:

TEMPERATURE:

LOCATION:

BIRD'S NAME:

NESTING:

COLOR AND MARKINGS:

BIRD'S BEHAVIOR:

MALE/FEMALE/NOT SURE

NUMBER OF BIRDS OBSERVED:

BIRD LOCATION

ground ☐

tree ☐

air ☐

bush ☐

feeder ☐

other:

NOTES

BIRD'S SKETCH

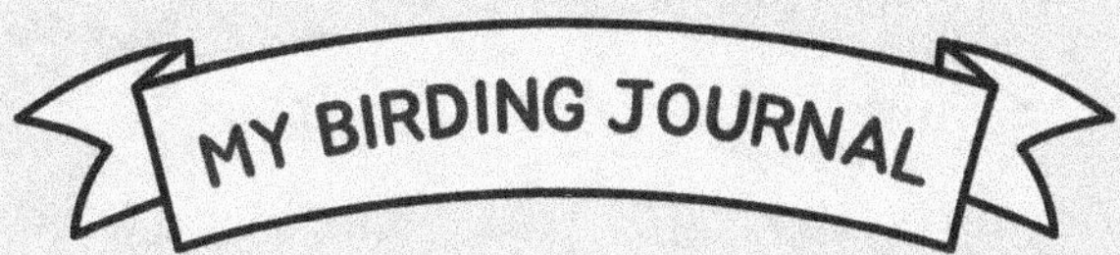

DATE:

SEASON:

WEATHER:

TIME:

HABITAT:

TEMPERATURE:

LOCATION:

BIRD'S NAME:	NESTING:
COLOR AND MARKINGS:	BIRD'S BEHAVIOR:
MALE/FEMALE/NOT SURE	NUMBER OF BIRDS OBSERVED:

BIRD LOCATION

ground ☐

tree ☐

air ☐

bush ☐

feeder ☐

other:

NOTES

BIRD'S SKETCH

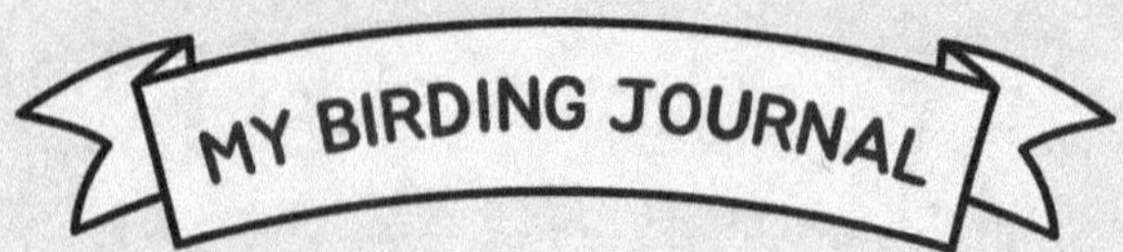

DATE:

SEASON:

WEATHER:

TIME:

HABITAT:

TEMPERATURE:

LOCATION:

BIRD'S NAME:	NESTING:
COLOR AND MARKINGS:	BIRD'S BEHAVIOR:
MALE/FEMALE/NOT SURE	NUMBER OF BIRDS OBSERVED:

BIRD LOCATION

ground ☐

tree ☐

air ☐

bush ☐

feeder ☐

other:

NOTES

BIRD'S SKETCH

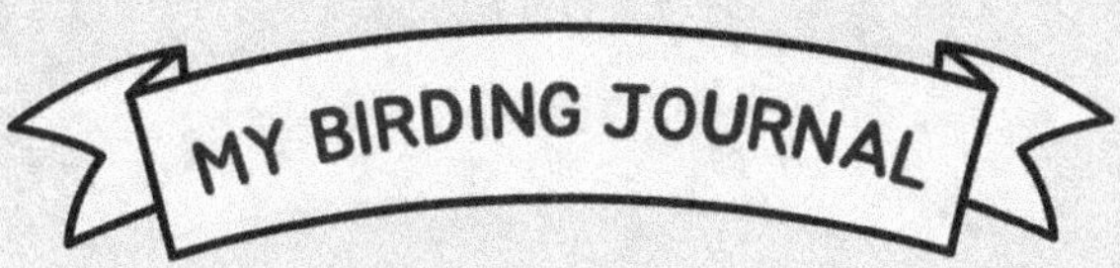

DATE:

SEASON:

WEATHER:

TIME:

HABITAT:

TEMPERATURE:

LOCATION:

BIRD'S NAME:	NESTING:
COLOR AND MARKINGS:	BIRD'S BEHAVIOR:
MALE/FEMALE/NOT SURE	NUMBER OF BIRDS OBSERVED:

BIRD LOCATION

ground ☐

tree ☐

air ☐

bush ☐

feeder ☐

other:

NOTES

BIRD'S SKETCH

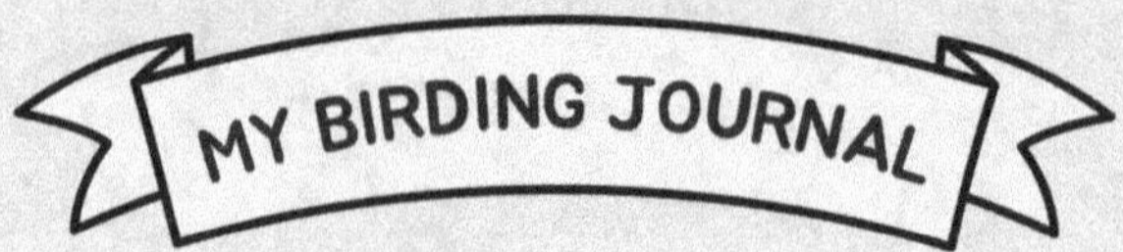

DATE:

SEASON:

WEATHER:

TIME:

HABITAT:

TEMPERATURE:

LOCATION:

BIRD'S NAME:	NESTING:
COLOR AND MARKINGS:	BIRD'S BEHAVIOR:
MALE/FEMALE/NOT SURE	NUMBER OF BIRDS OBSERVED:

BIRD LOCATION

ground ☐

tree ☐

air ☐

bush ☐

feeder ☐

other:

NOTES

BIRD'S SKETCH

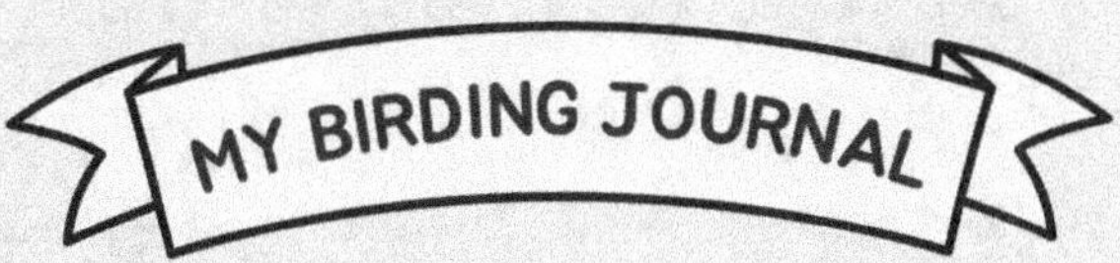

DATE:

SEASON:

WEATHER:

TIME:

HABITAT:

TEMPERATURE:

LOCATION:

BIRD'S NAME:

NESTING:

COLOR AND MARKINGS:

BIRD'S BEHAVIOR:

MALE/FEMALE/NOT SURE

NUMBER OF BIRDS OBSERVED:

BIRD LOCATION

ground ☐

tree ☐

air ☐

bush ☐

feeder ☐

other:

NOTES

BIRD'S SKETCH

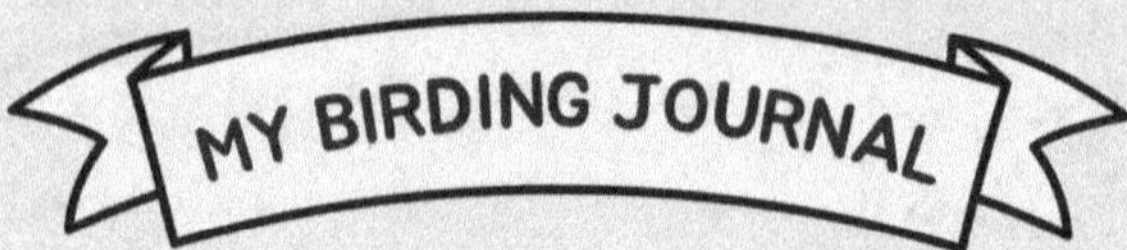

DATE:

SEASON:

WEATHER:

TIME:

HABITAT:

TEMPERATURE:

LOCATION:

BIRD'S NAME:

NESTING:

COLOR AND MARKINGS:

BIRD'S BEHAVIOR:

MALE/FEMALE/NOT SURE

NUMBER OF BIRDS OBSERVED:

BIRD LOCATION

ground ☐

tree ☐

air ☐

bush ☐

feeder ☐

other:

NOTES

BIRD'S SKETCH

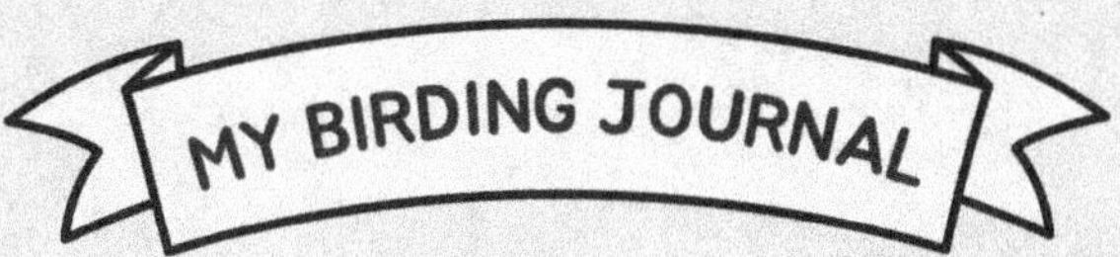

DATE:

SEASON:

WEATHER:

TIME:

HABITAT:

TEMPERATURE:

LOCATION:

BIRD'S NAME:	NESTING:
COLOR AND MARKINGS:	BIRD'S BEHAVIOR:
MALE/FEMALE/NOT SURE	NUMBER OF BIRDS OBSERVED:

BIRD LOCATION

ground ☐

tree ☐

air ☐

bush ☐

feeder ☐

other:

NOTES

BIRD'S SKETCH

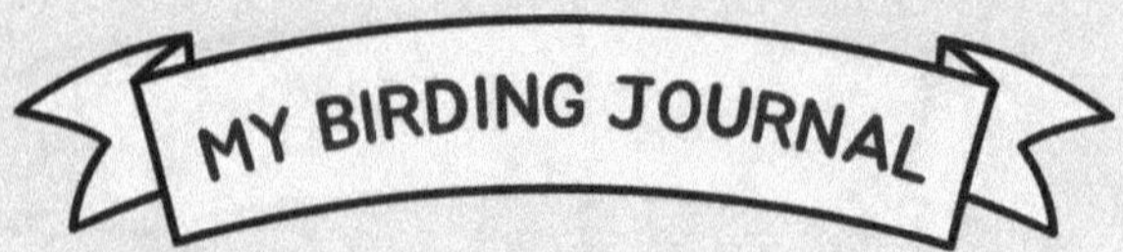

DATE:

SEASON:

WEATHER:

TIME:

HABITAT:

TEMPERATURE:

LOCATION:

BIRD'S NAME:

NESTING:

COLOR AND MARKINGS:

BIRD'S BEHAVIOR:

MALE/FEMALE/NOT SURE

NUMBER OF BIRDS OBSERVED:

BIRD LOCATION

ground ☐

tree ☐

air ☐

bush ☐

feeder ☐

other:

NOTES

BIRD'S SKETCH

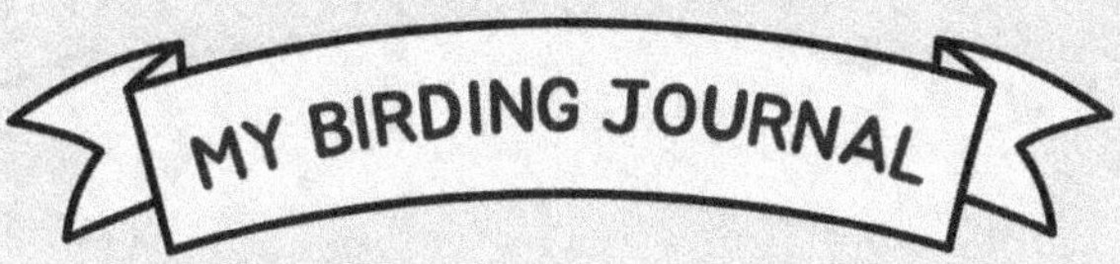

DATE:

SEASON:

WEATHER:

TIME:

HABITAT:

TEMPERATURE:

LOCATION:

BIRD'S NAME:

NESTING:

COLOR AND MARKINGS:

BIRD'S BEHAVIOR:

MALE/FEMALE/NOT SURE

NUMBER OF BIRDS OBSERVED:

BIRD LOCATION

ground ☐

tree ☐

air ☐

bush ☐

feeder ☐

other:

NOTES

BIRD'S SKETCH

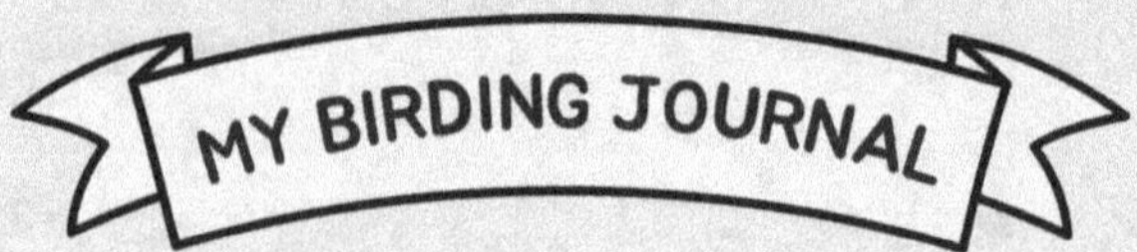

DATE:

SEASON:

WEATHER:

TIME:

HABITAT:

TEMPERATURE:

LOCATION:

BIRD'S NAME:

NESTING:

COLOR AND MARKINGS:

BIRD'S BEHAVIOR:

MALE/FEMALE/NOT SURE

NUMBER OF BIRDS OBSERVED:

BIRD LOCATION

ground

tree

air

bush

feeder

other:

NOTES

BIRD'S SKETCH

28

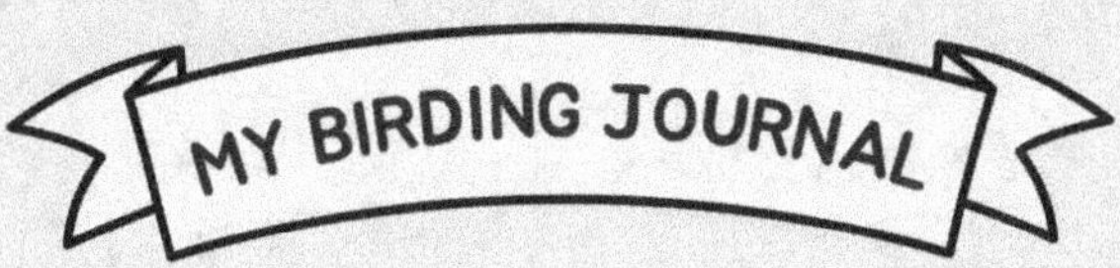

DATE:

SEASON:

WEATHER:

TIME:

HABITAT:

TEMPERATURE:

LOCATION:

BIRD'S NAME:

NESTING:

COLOR AND MARKINGS:

BIRD'S BEHAVIOR:

MALE/FEMALE/NOT SURE

NUMBER OF BIRDS OBSERVED:

BIRD LOCATION

ground ☐

tree ☐

air ☐

bush ☐

feeder ☐

other:

NOTES

BIRD'S SKETCH

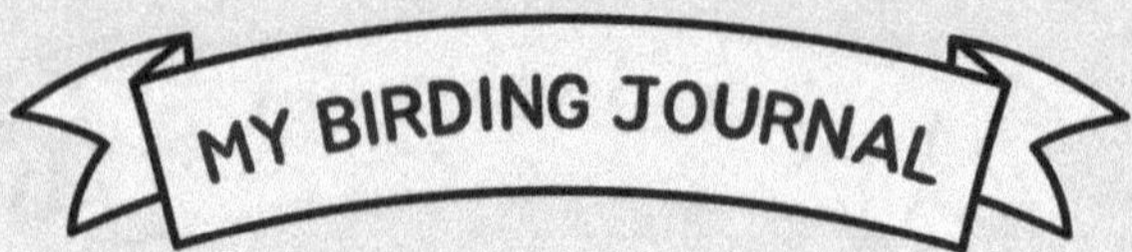

DATE:

SEASON:

WEATHER:

TIME:

HABITAT:

TEMPERATURE:

LOCATION:

BIRD'S NAME:

NESTING:

COLOR AND MARKINGS:

BIRD'S BEHAVIOR:

MALE/FEMALE/NOT SURE

NUMBER OF BIRDS OBSERVED:

BIRD LOCATION

ground ☐

tree ☐

air ☐

bush ☐

feeder ☐

other:

NOTES

BIRD'S SKETCH

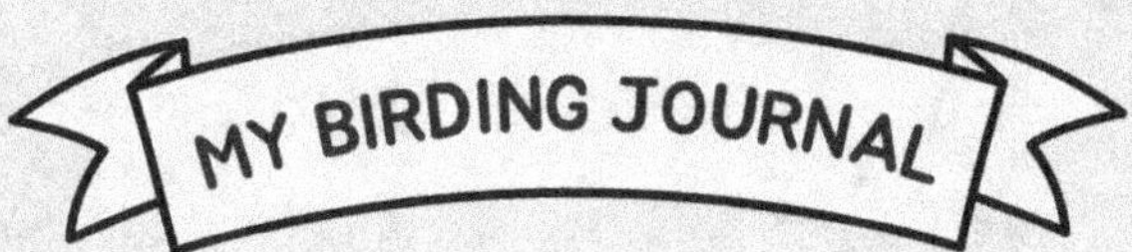

DATE:

SEASON:

WEATHER:

TIME:

HABITAT:

TEMPERATURE:

LOCATION:

BIRD'S NAME:

NESTING:

COLOR AND MARKINGS:

BIRD'S BEHAVIOR:

MALE/FEMALE/NOT SURE

NUMBER OF BIRDS OBSERVED:

BIRD LOCATION

ground ☐

tree ☐

air ☐

bush ☐

feeder ☐

other:

NOTES

BIRD'S SKETCH

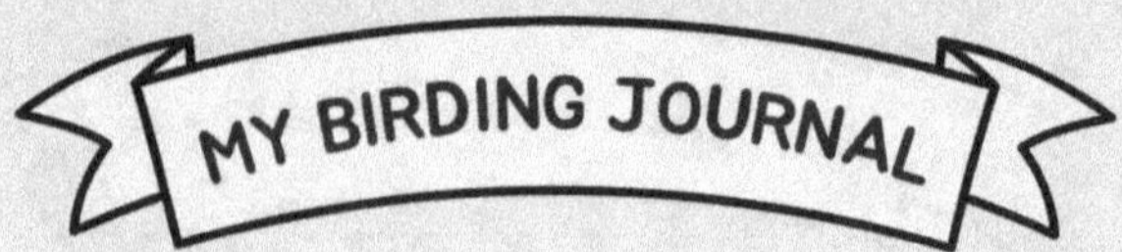

DATE:

SEASON:

WEATHER:

TIME:

HABITAT:

TEMPERATURE:

LOCATION:

BIRD'S NAME:	NESTING:
COLOR AND MARKINGS:	BIRD'S BEHAVIOR:
MALE/FEMALE/NOT SURE	NUMBER OF BIRDS OBSERVED:

BIRD LOCATION

ground ☐

tree ☐

air ☐

bush ☐

feeder ☐

other:

NOTES

BIRD'S SKETCH

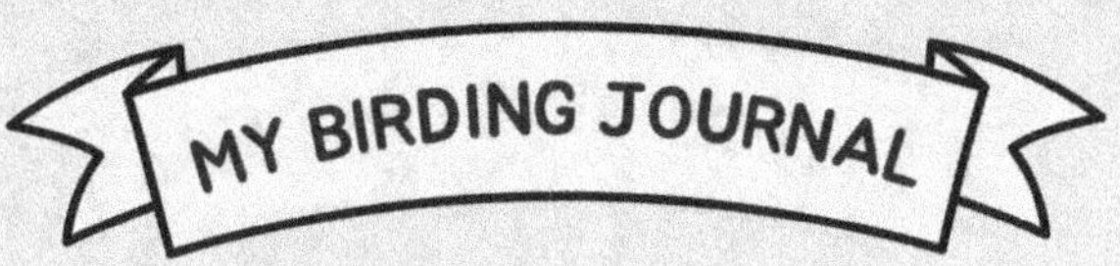

DATE:

SEASON:

WEATHER:

TIME:

HABITAT:

TEMPERATURE:

LOCATION:

BIRD'S NAME:

NESTING:

COLOR AND MARKINGS:

BIRD'S BEHAVIOR:

MALE/FEMALE/NOT SURE

NUMBER OF BIRDS OBSERVED:

BIRD LOCATION

ground ☐

tree ☐

air ☐

bush ☐

feeder ☐

other:

NOTES

BIRD'S SKETCH

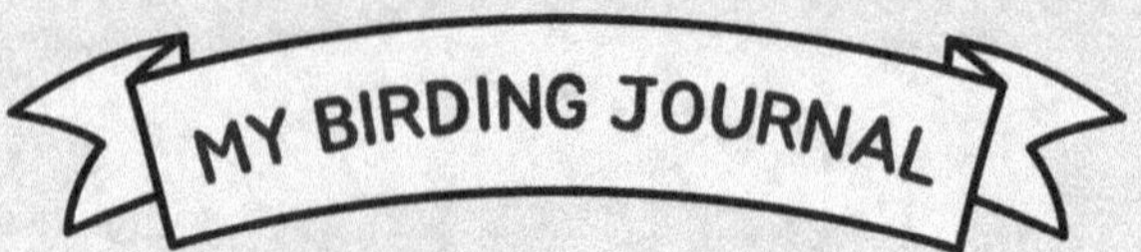

DATE:

SEASON:

WEATHER:

TIME:

HABITAT:

TEMPERATURE:

LOCATION:

BIRD'S NAME:

NESTING:

COLOR AND MARKINGS:

BIRD'S BEHAVIOR:

MALE/FEMALE/NOT SURE

NUMBER OF BIRDS OBSERVED:

BIRD LOCATION

ground ☐
tree ☐
air ☐
bush ☐
feeder ☐
other:

NOTES

BIRD'S SKETCH

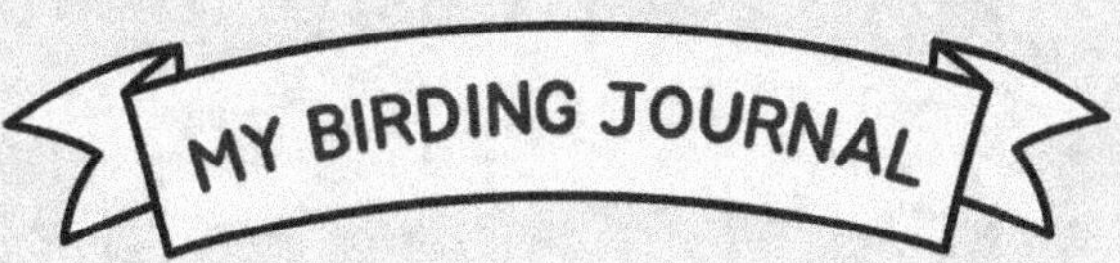

DATE:

SEASON:

WEATHER:

TIME:

HABITAT:

TEMPERATURE:

LOCATION:

BIRD'S NAME:	NESTING:
COLOR AND MARKINGS:	BIRD'S BEHAVIOR:
MALE/FEMALE/NOT SURE	NUMBER OF BIRDS OBSERVED:

BIRD LOCATION

ground ☐

tree ☐

air ☐

bush ☐

feeder ☐

other:

NOTES

BIRD'S SKETCH

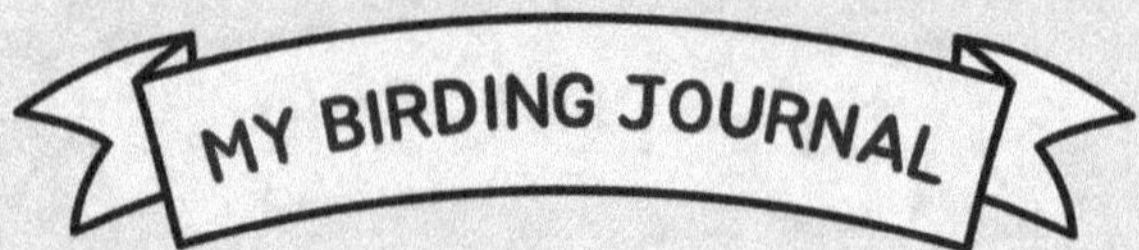

DATE:

SEASON:

WEATHER:

TIME:

HABITAT:

TEMPERATURE:

LOCATION:

BIRD'S NAME:

NESTING:

COLOR AND MARKINGS:

BIRD'S BEHAVIOR:

MALE/FEMALE/NOT SURE

NUMBER OF BIRDS OBSERVED:

BIRD LOCATION

ground

tree

air

bush

feeder

other:

NOTES

BIRD'S SKETCH

DATE:

SEASON:

WEATHER:

TIME:

HABITAT:

TEMPERATURE:

LOCATION:

BIRD'S NAME:

NESTING:

COLOR AND MARKINGS:

BIRD'S BEHAVIOR:

MALE/FEMALE/NOT SURE

NUMBER OF BIRDS OBSERVED:

BIRD LOCATION

ground ☐
tree ☐
air ☐
bush ☐
feeder ☐
other:

NOTES

BIRD'S SKETCH

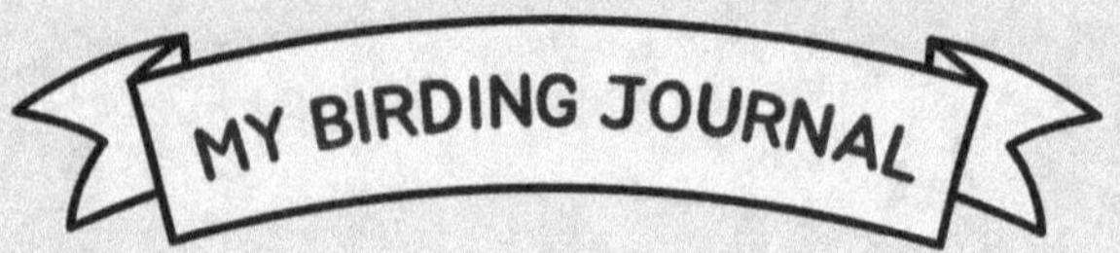

DATE:

SEASON:

WEATHER:

TIME:

HABITAT:

TEMPERATURE:

LOCATION:

BIRD'S NAME:	NESTING:
COLOR AND MARKINGS:	BIRD'S BEHAVIOR:
MALE/FEMALE/NOT SURE	NUMBER OF BIRDS OBSERVED:

BIRD LOCATION

ground ☐

tree ☐

air ☐

bush ☐

feeder ☐

other:

NOTES

BIRD'S SKETCH

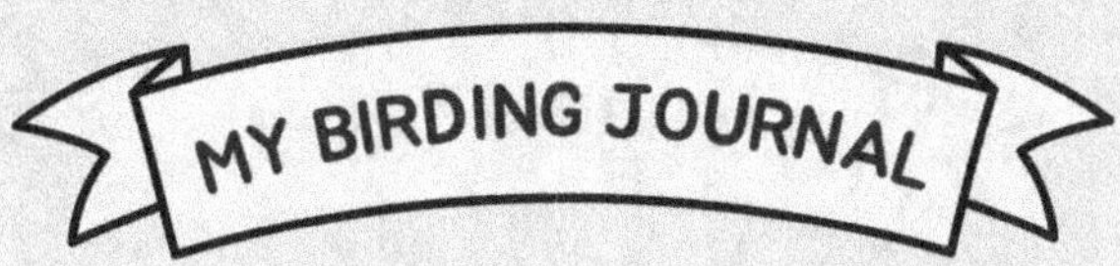

DATE:

SEASON:

WEATHER:

TIME:

HABITAT:

TEMPERATURE:

LOCATION:

BIRD'S NAME:

NESTING:

COLOR AND MARKINGS:

BIRD'S BEHAVIOR:

MALE/FEMALE/NOT SURE

NUMBER OF BIRDS OBSERVED:

BIRD LOCATION

ground ☐

tree ☐

air ☐

bush ☐

feeder ☐

other:

NOTES

BIRD'S SKETCH

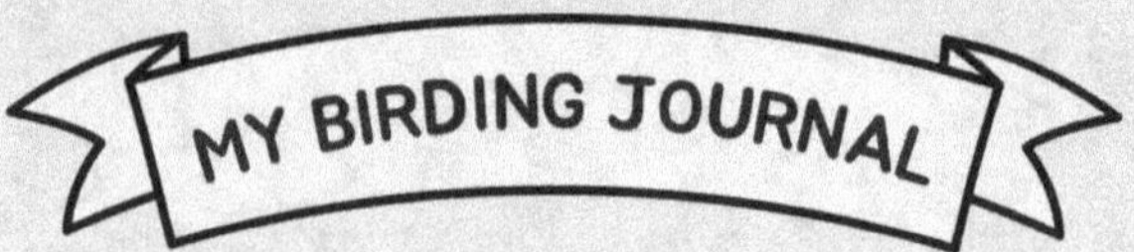

DATE:

SEASON:

WEATHER:

TIME:

HABITAT:

TEMPERATURE:

LOCATION:

BIRD'S NAME:

NESTING:

COLOR AND MARKINGS:

BIRD'S BEHAVIOR:

MALE/FEMALE/NOT SURE

NUMBER OF BIRDS OBSERVED:

BIRD LOCATION

ground ☐
tree ☐
air ☐
bush ☐
feeder ☐
other:

NOTES

BIRD'S SKETCH

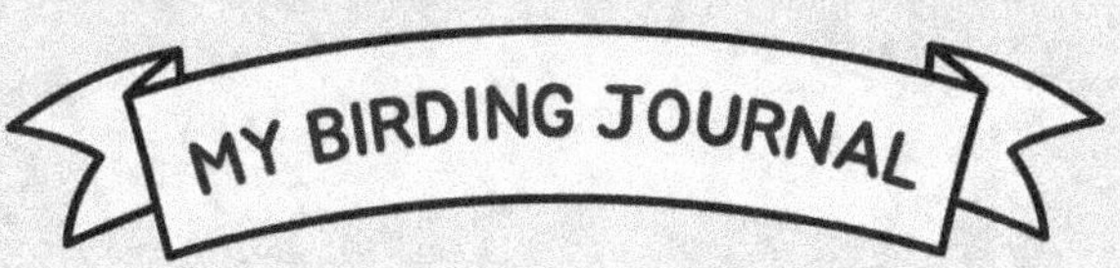

DATE:

SEASON:

WEATHER:

TIME:

HABITAT:

TEMPERATURE:

LOCATION:

BIRD'S NAME:	NESTING:
COLOR AND MARKINGS:	BIRD'S BEHAVIOR:
MALE/FEMALE/NOT SURE	NUMBER OF BIRDS OBSERVED:

BIRD LOCATION

ground ☐

tree ☐

air ☐

bush ☐

feeder ☐

other:

NOTES

BIRD'S SKETCH

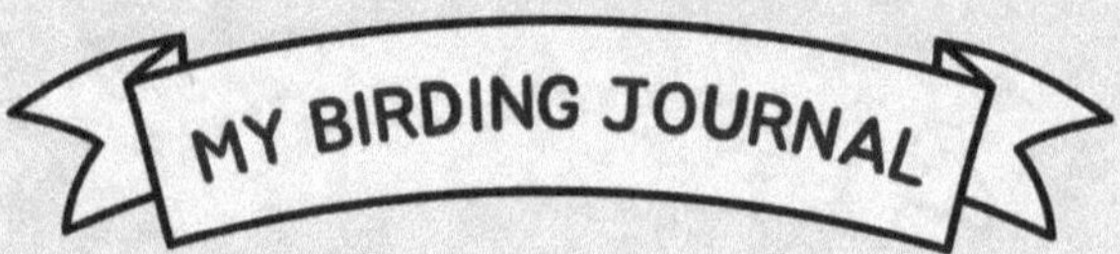

DATE:

SEASON:

WEATHER:

TIME:

HABITAT:

TEMPERATURE:

LOCATION:

BIRD'S NAME:

NESTING:

COLOR AND MARKINGS:

BIRD'S BEHAVIOR:

MALE/FEMALE/NOT SURE

NUMBER OF BIRDS OBSERVED:

BIRD LOCATION

ground ☐

tree ☐

air ☐

bush ☐

feeder ☐

other:

NOTES

BIRD'S SKETCH

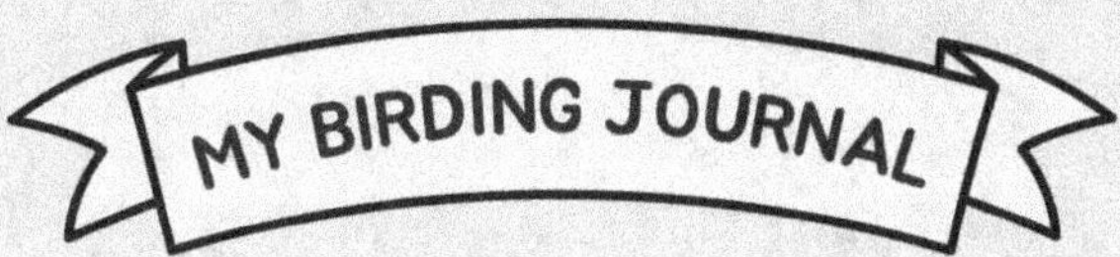

DATE:

SEASON:

WEATHER:

TIME:

HABITAT:

TEMPERATURE:

LOCATION:

BIRD'S NAME:

NESTING:

COLOR AND MARKINGS:

BIRD'S BEHAVIOR:

MALE/FEMALE/NOT SURE

NUMBER OF BIRDS OBSERVED:

BIRD LOCATION

ground ☐

tree ☐

air ☐

bush ☐

feeder ☐

other:

NOTES

BIRD'S SKETCH

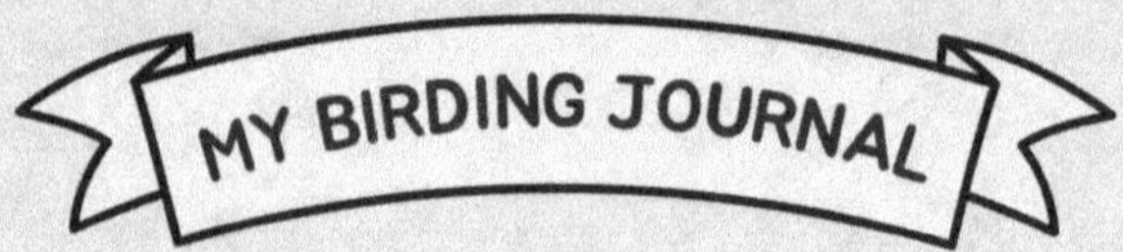

DATE:

SEASON:

WEATHER:

TIME:

HABITAT:

TEMPERATURE:

LOCATION:

BIRD'S NAME:

NESTING:

COLOR AND MARKINGS:

BIRD'S BEHAVIOR:

MALE/FEMALE/NOT SURE

NUMBER OF BIRDS OBSERVED:

BIRD LOCATION

ground ☐

tree ☐

air ☐

bush ☐

feeder ☐

other:

NOTES

BIRD'S SKETCH

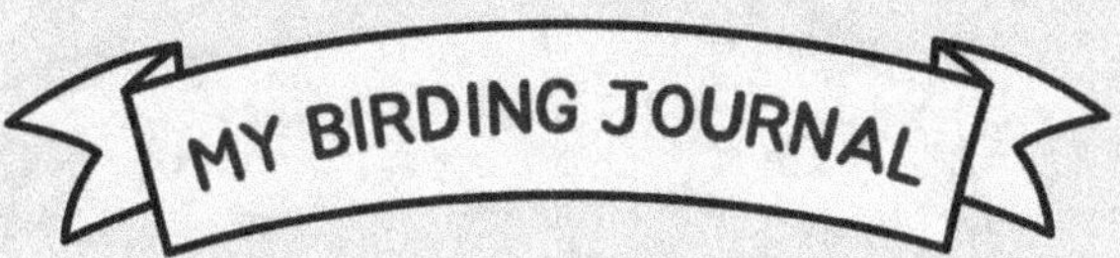

DATE:

SEASON:

WEATHER:

TIME:

HABITAT:

TEMPERATURE:

LOCATION:

BIRD'S NAME:	NESTING:
COLOR AND MARKINGS:	BIRD'S BEHAVIOR:
MALE/FEMALE/NOT SURE	NUMBER OF BIRDS OBSERVED:

BIRD LOCATION

ground ☐

tree ☐

air ☐

bush ☐

feeder ☐

other:

NOTES

BIRD'S SKETCH

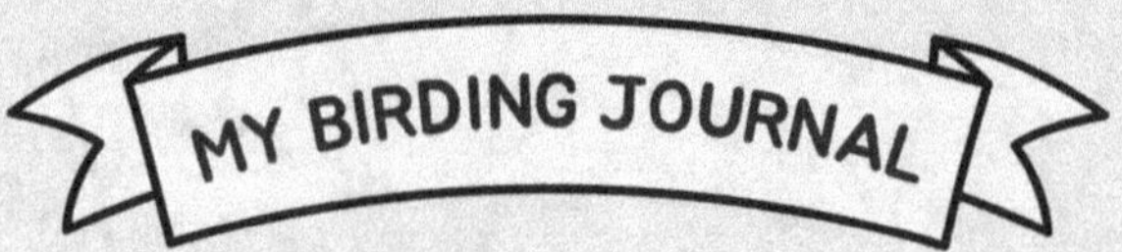

DATE:

SEASON:

WEATHER:

TIME:

HABITAT:

TEMPERATURE:

LOCATION:

BIRD'S NAME:

NESTING:

COLOR AND MARKINGS:

BIRD'S BEHAVIOR:

MALE/FEMALE/NOT SURE

NUMBER OF BIRDS OBSERVED:

BIRD LOCATION

- ground ☐
- tree ☐
- air ☐
- bush ☐
- feeder ☐
- other:

NOTES

BIRD'S SKETCH

DATE:

SEASON:

WEATHER:

TIME:

HABITAT:

TEMPERATURE:

LOCATION:

BIRD'S NAME:

NESTING:

COLOR AND MARKINGS:

BIRD'S BEHAVIOR:

MALE/FEMALE/NOT SURE

NUMBER OF BIRDS OBSERVED:

BIRD LOCATION

ground ☐

tree ☐

air ☐

bush ☐

feeder ☐

other:

NOTES

BIRD'S SKETCH

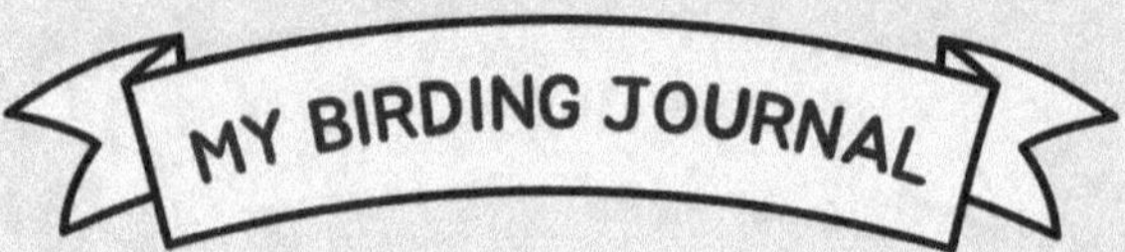

DATE:

SEASON:

WEATHER:

TIME:

HABITAT:

TEMPERATURE:

LOCATION:

BIRD'S NAME:

NESTING:

COLOR AND MARKINGS:

BIRD'S BEHAVIOR:

MALE/FEMALE/NOT SURE

NUMBER OF BIRDS OBSERVED:

BIRD LOCATION

ground

tree

air

bush

feeder

other:

NOTES

BIRD'S SKETCH

DATE:

SEASON:

WEATHER:

TIME:

HABITAT:

TEMPERATURE:

LOCATION:

BIRD'S NAME:	NESTING:
COLOR AND MARKINGS:	BIRD'S BEHAVIOR:
MALE/FEMALE/NOT SURE	NUMBER OF BIRDS OBSERVED:

BIRD LOCATION

ground ☐

tree ☐

air ☐

bush ☐

feeder ☐

other:

NOTES

BIRD'S SKETCH

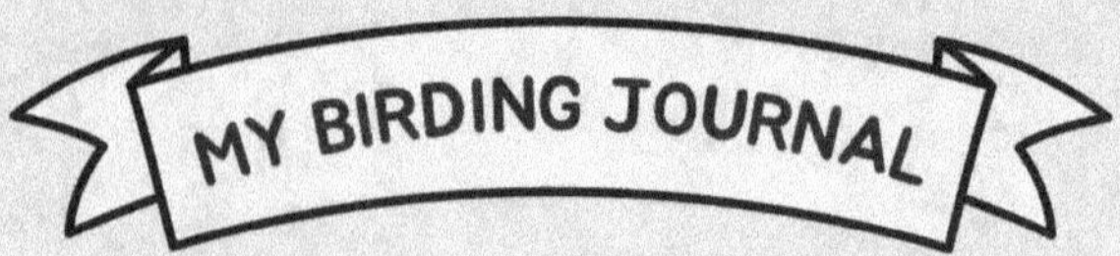

DATE:

SEASON:

WEATHER:

TIME:

HABITAT:

TEMPERATURE:

LOCATION:

BIRD'S NAME:

NESTING:

COLOR AND MARKINGS:

BIRD'S BEHAVIOR:

MALE/FEMALE/NOT SURE

NUMBER OF BIRDS OBSERVED:

BIRD LOCATION

ground ☐

tree ☐

air ☐

bush ☐

feeder ☐

other:

NOTES

BIRD'S SKETCH

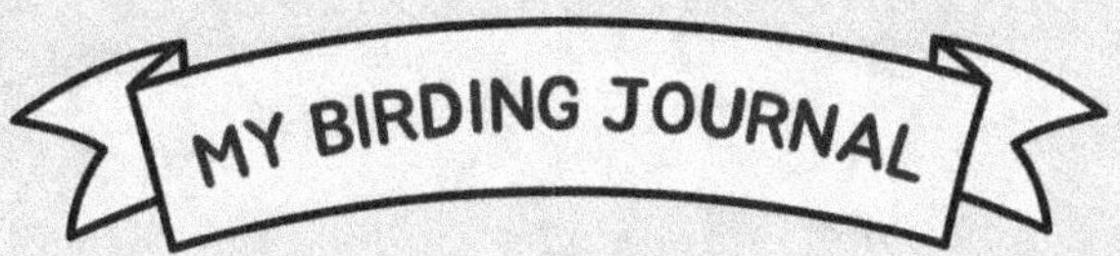

DATE:

SEASON:

WEATHER:

TIME:

HABITAT:

TEMPERATURE:

LOCATION:

BIRD'S NAME:

NESTING:

COLOR AND MARKINGS:

BIRD'S BEHAVIOR:

MALE/FEMALE/NOT SURE

NUMBER OF BIRDS OBSERVED:

BIRD LOCATION

ground ☐

tree ☐

air ☐

bush ☐

feeder ☐

other:

NOTES

BIRD'S SKETCH

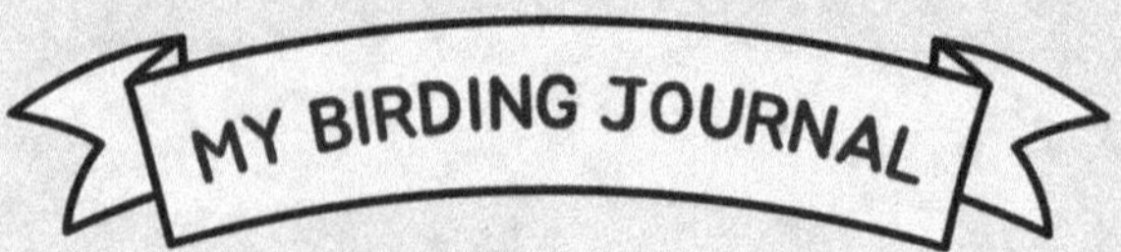

DATE:

SEASON:

WEATHER:

TIME:

HABITAT:

TEMPERATURE:

LOCATION:

BIRD'S NAME:

NESTING:

COLOR AND MARKINGS:

BIRD'S BEHAVIOR:

MALE/FEMALE/NOT SURE

NUMBER OF BIRDS OBSERVED:

BIRD LOCATION

ground

tree

air

bush

feeder

other:

NOTES

BIRD'S SKETCH

DATE:

SEASON:

WEATHER:

TIME:

HABITAT:

TEMPERATURE:

LOCATION:

BIRD'S NAME:

NESTING:

COLOR AND MARKINGS:

BIRD'S BEHAVIOR:

MALE/FEMALE/NOT SURE

NUMBER OF BIRDS OBSERVED:

BIRD LOCATION

ground ☐
tree ☐
air ☐
bush ☐
feeder ☐
other:

NOTES

BIRD'S SKETCH

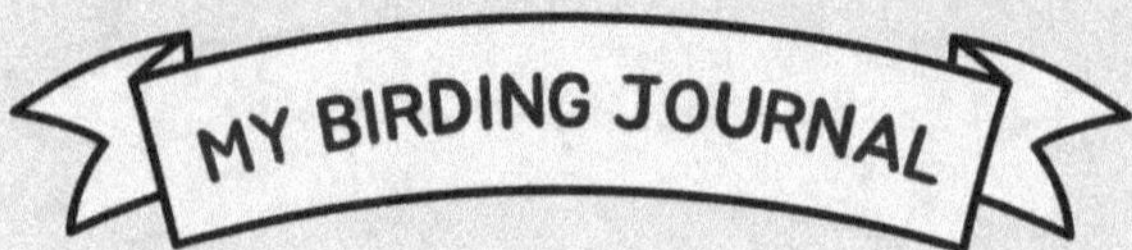

DATE:

SEASON:

WEATHER:

TIME:

HABITAT:

TEMPERATURE:

LOCATION:

BIRD'S NAME:

NESTING:

COLOR AND MARKINGS:

BIRD'S BEHAVIOR:

MALE/FEMALE/NOT SURE

NUMBER OF BIRDS OBSERVED:

BIRD LOCATION

ground

tree

air

bush

feeder

other:

NOTES

BIRD'S SKETCH

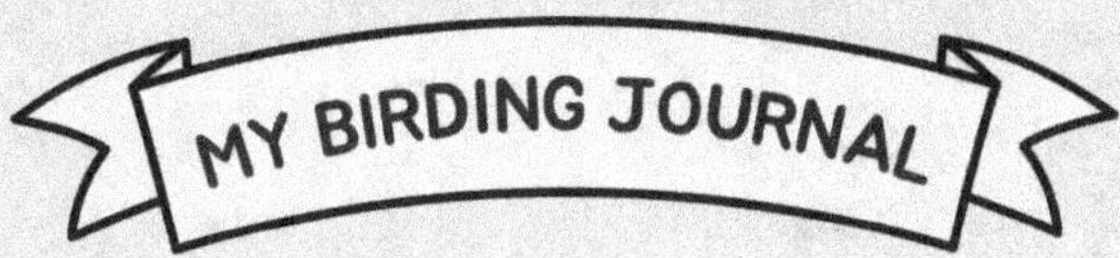

DATE:

SEASON:

WEATHER:

TIME:

HABITAT:

TEMPERATURE:

LOCATION:

BIRD'S NAME:

NESTING:

COLOR AND MARKINGS:

BIRD'S BEHAVIOR:

MALE/FEMALE/NOT SURE

NUMBER OF BIRDS OBSERVED:

BIRD LOCATION

ground ☐
tree ☐
air ☐
bush ☐
feeder ☐
other:

NOTES

BIRD'S SKETCH

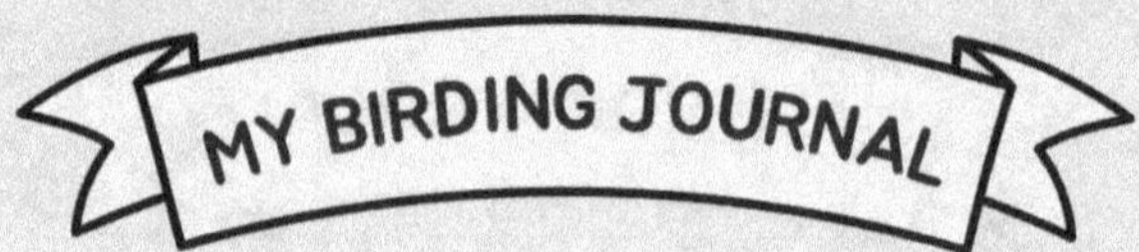

DATE:

SEASON:

WEATHER:

TIME:

HABITAT:

TEMPERATURE:

LOCATION:

BIRD'S NAME:

NESTING:

COLOR AND MARKINGS:

BIRD'S BEHAVIOR:

MALE/FEMALE/NOT SURE

NUMBER OF BIRDS OBSERVED:

BIRD LOCATION

ground

tree

air

bush

feeder

other:

NOTES

BIRD'S SKETCH

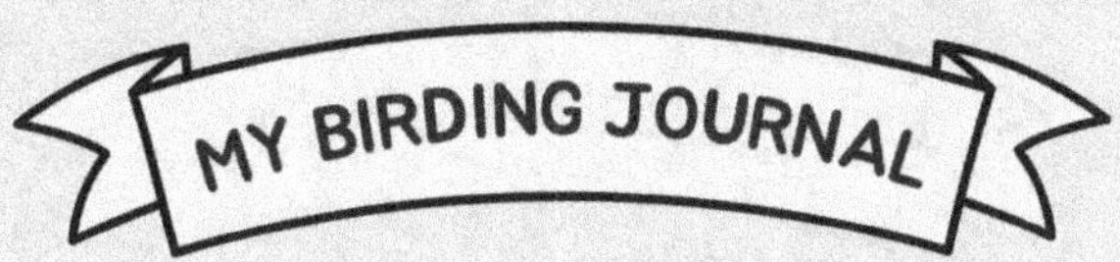

DATE:

SEASON:

WEATHER:

TIME:

HABITAT:

TEMPERATURE:

LOCATION:

BIRD'S NAME:

NESTING:

COLOR AND MARKINGS:

BIRD'S BEHAVIOR:

MALE/FEMALE/NOT SURE

NUMBER OF BIRDS OBSERVED:

BIRD LOCATION

ground ☐
tree ☐
air ☐
bush ☐
feeder ☐
other:

NOTES

BIRD'S SKETCH

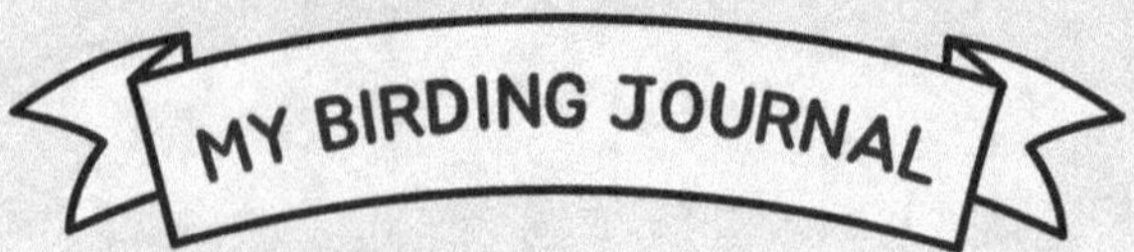

DATE:

SEASON:

WEATHER:

TIME:

HABITAT:

TEMPERATURE:

LOCATION:

BIRD'S NAME:

NESTING:

COLOR AND MARKINGS:

BIRD'S BEHAVIOR:

MALE/FEMALE/NOT SURE

NUMBER OF BIRDS OBSERVED:

BIRD LOCATION

ground ☐
tree ☐
air ☐
bush ☐
feeder ☐
other:

NOTES

BIRD'S SKETCH

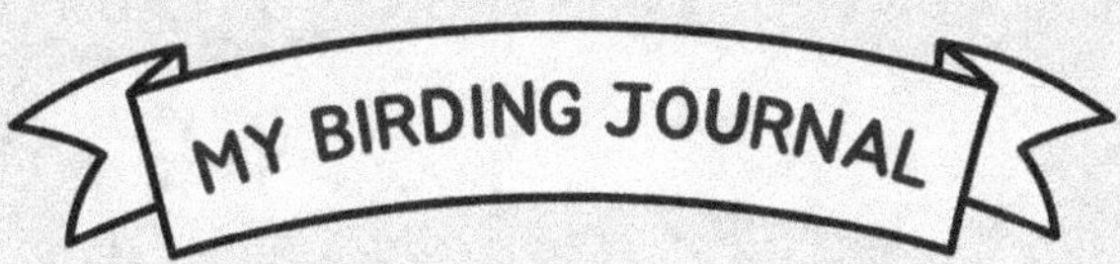

DATE:

SEASON:

WEATHER:

TIME:

HABITAT:

TEMPERATURE:

LOCATION:

BIRD'S NAME:

NESTING:

COLOR AND MARKINGS:

BIRD'S BEHAVIOR:

MALE/FEMALE/NOT SURE

NUMBER OF BIRDS OBSERVED:

BIRD LOCATION

ground ☐

tree ☐

air ☐

bush ☐

feeder ☐

other:

NOTES

BIRD'S SKETCH

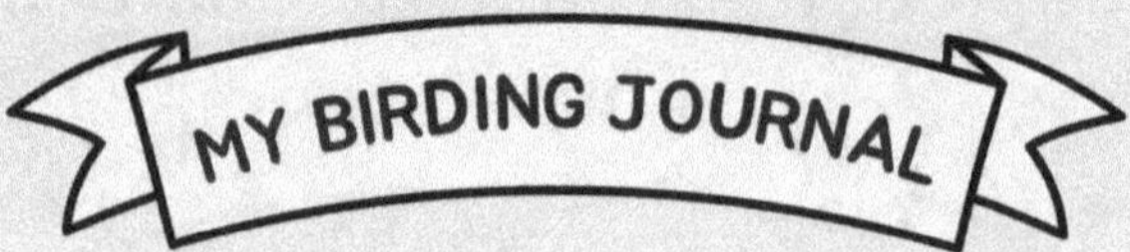

DATE:

SEASON:

WEATHER:

TIME:

HABITAT:

TEMPERATURE:

LOCATION:

BIRD'S NAME:

NESTING:

COLOR AND MARKINGS:

BIRD'S BEHAVIOR:

MALE/FEMALE/NOT SURE

NUMBER OF BIRDS OBSERVED:

BIRD LOCATION

ground ☐

tree ☐

air ☐

bush ☐

feeder ☐

other:

NOTES

BIRD'S SKETCH

DATE:

SEASON:

WEATHER:

TIME:

HABITAT:

TEMPERATURE:

LOCATION:

BIRD'S NAME:	NESTING:
COLOR AND MARKINGS:	BIRD'S BEHAVIOR:
MALE/FEMALE/NOT SURE	NUMBER OF BIRDS OBSERVED:

BIRD LOCATION

ground ☐

tree ☐

air ☐

bush ☐

feeder ☐

other:

NOTES

BIRD'S SKETCH

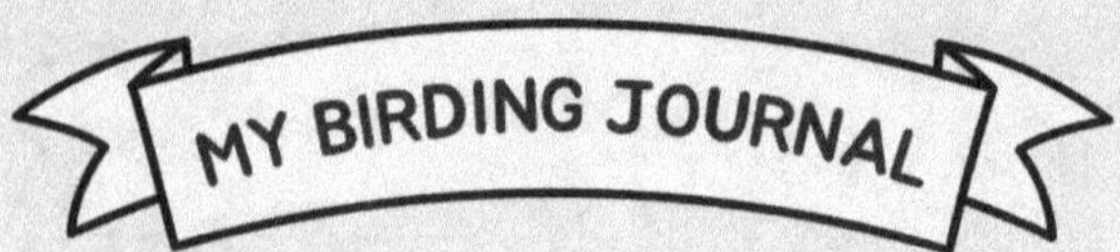

DATE:

SEASON:

WEATHER:

TIME:

HABITAT:

TEMPERATURE:

LOCATION:

BIRD'S NAME:

NESTING:

COLOR AND MARKINGS:

BIRD'S BEHAVIOR:

MALE/FEMALE/NOT SURE

NUMBER OF BIRDS OBSERVED:

BIRD LOCATION

ground

tree

air

bush

feeder

other:

NOTES

BIRD'S SKETCH

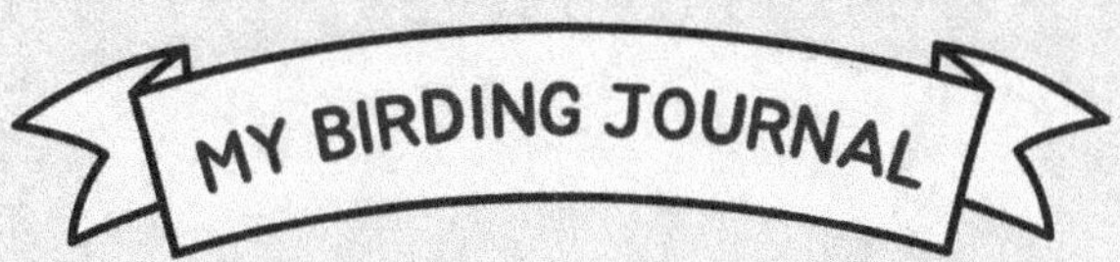

DATE:

SEASON:

WEATHER:

TIME:

HABITAT:

TEMPERATURE:

LOCATION:

BIRD'S NAME:	NESTING:
COLOR AND MARKINGS:	BIRD'S BEHAVIOR:
MALE/FEMALE/NOT SURE	NUMBER OF BIRDS OBSERVED:

BIRD LOCATION

ground ☐

tree ☐

air ☐

bush ☐

feeder ☐

other:

NOTES

BIRD'S SKETCH

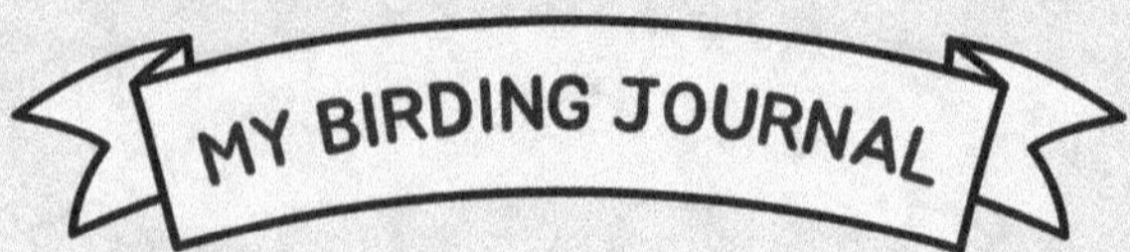

DATE:

SEASON:

WEATHER:

TIME:

HABITAT:

TEMPERATURE:

LOCATION:

BIRD'S NAME:

NESTING:

COLOR AND MARKINGS:

BIRD'S BEHAVIOR:

MALE/FEMALE/NOT SURE

NUMBER OF BIRDS OBSERVED:

BIRD LOCATION

ground ☐

tree ☐

air ☐

bush ☐

feeder ☐

other:

NOTES

BIRD'S SKETCH

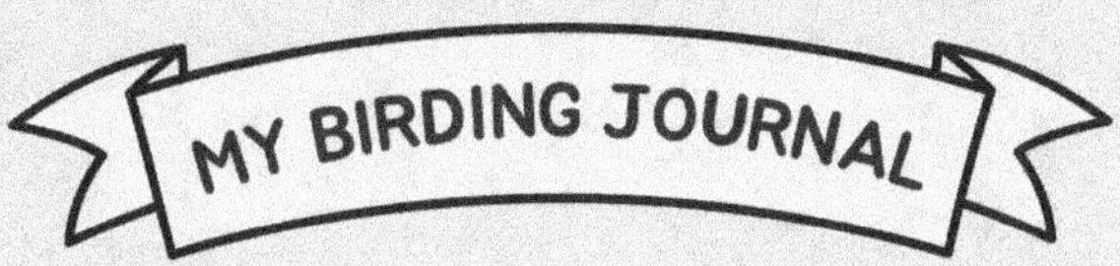

DATE:

TIME:

TEMPERATURE:

SEASON:

HABITAT:

LOCATION:

WEATHER:

BIRD'S NAME:

COLOR AND MARKINGS:

MALE/FEMALE/NOT SURE

NESTING:

BIRD'S BEHAVIOR:

NUMBER OF BIRDS OBSERVED:

BIRD LOCATION

ground ☐
tree ☐
air ☐
bush ☐
feeder ☐
other:

NOTES

BIRD'S SKETCH

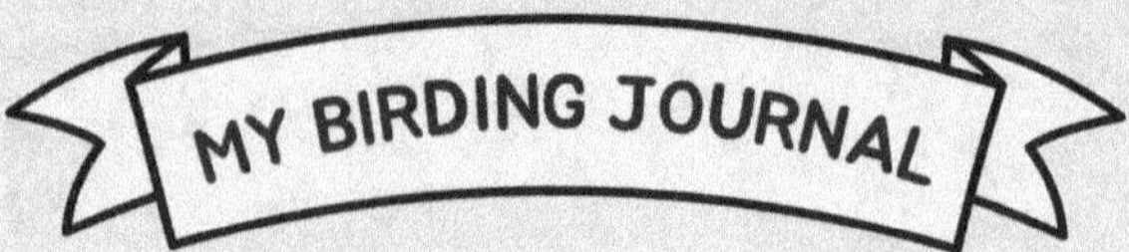

DATE:

SEASON:

WEATHER:

TIME:

HABITAT:

TEMPERATURE:

LOCATION:

BIRD'S NAME:

NESTING:

COLOR AND MARKINGS:

BIRD'S BEHAVIOR:

MALE/FEMALE/NOT SURE

NUMBER OF BIRDS OBSERVED:

BIRD LOCATION

ground ☐

tree ☐

air ☐

bush ☐

feeder ☐

other:

NOTES

BIRD'S SKETCH

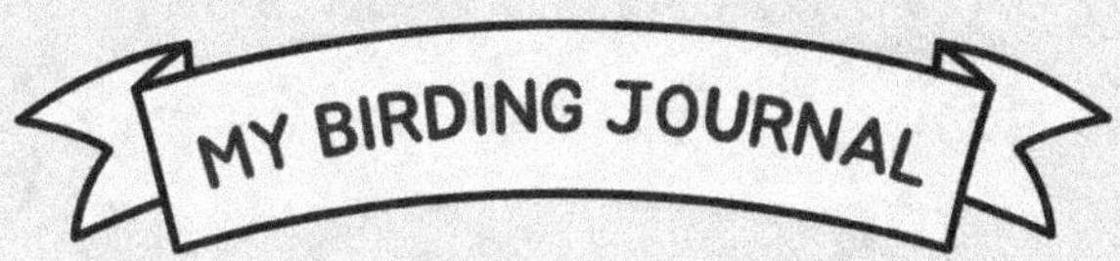

DATE:

SEASON:

WEATHER:

TIME:

HABITAT:

TEMPERATURE:

LOCATION:

BIRD'S NAME:

NESTING:

COLOR AND MARKINGS:

BIRD'S BEHAVIOR:

MALE/FEMALE/NOT SURE

NUMBER OF BIRDS OBSERVED:

BIRD LOCATION

ground ☐
tree ☐
air ☐
bush ☐
feeder ☐
other:

NOTES

BIRD'S SKETCH

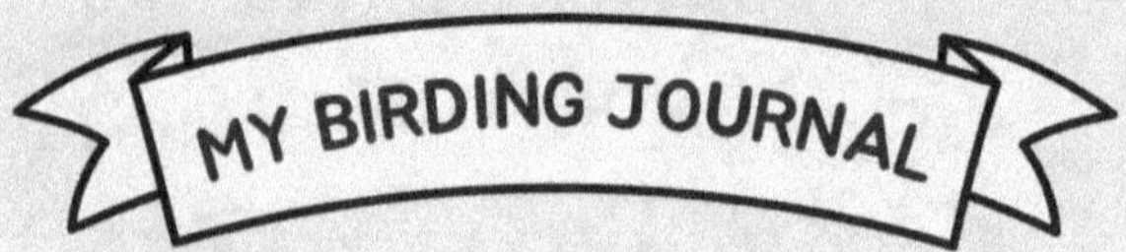

DATE:

SEASON:

WEATHER:

TIME:

HABITAT:

TEMPERATURE:

LOCATION:

BIRD'S NAME:	NESTING:
COLOR AND MARKINGS:	BIRD'S BEHAVIOR:
MALE/FEMALE/NOT SURE	NUMBER OF BIRDS OBSERVED:

BIRD LOCATION

ground ☐

tree ☐

air ☐

bush ☐

feeder ☐

other:

NOTES

BIRD'S SKETCH

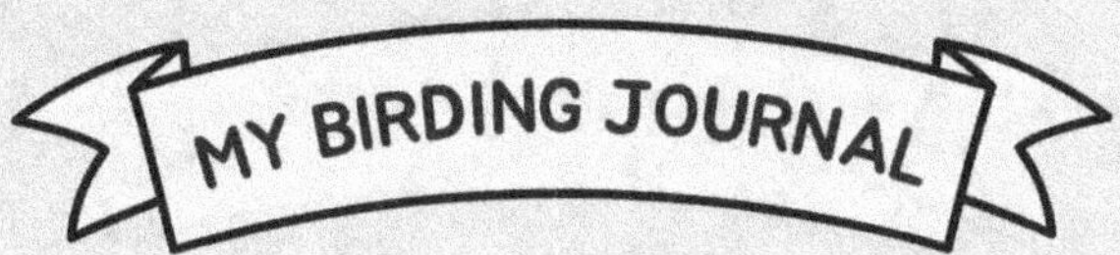

DATE:

SEASON:

WEATHER:

TIME:

HABITAT:

TEMPERATURE:

LOCATION:

BIRD'S NAME:	NESTING:
COLOR AND MARKINGS:	BIRD'S BEHAVIOR:
MALE/FEMALE/NOT SURE	NUMBER OF BIRDS OBSERVED:

BIRD LOCATION

ground

tree

air

bush

feeder

other:

NOTES

BIRD'S SKETCH

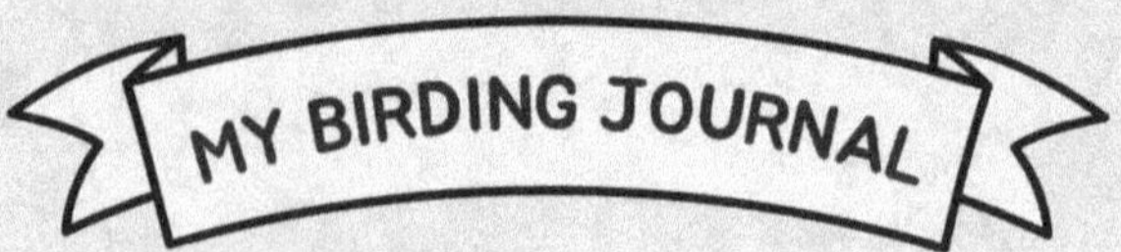

DATE:

SEASON:

WEATHER:

TIME:

HABITAT:

TEMPERATURE:

LOCATION:

BIRD'S NAME:

NESTING:

COLOR AND MARKINGS:

BIRD'S BEHAVIOR:

MALE/FEMALE/NOT SURE

NUMBER OF BIRDS OBSERVED:

BIRD LOCATION

ground ☐

tree ☐

air ☐

bush ☐

feeder ☐

other:

NOTES

BIRD'S SKETCH

DATE:

SEASON:

WEATHER:

TIME:

HABITAT:

TEMPERATURE:

LOCATION:

BIRD'S NAME:	NESTING:
COLOR AND MARKINGS:	BIRD'S BEHAVIOR:
MALE/FEMALE/NOT SURE	NUMBER OF BIRDS OBSERVED:

BIRD LOCATION

ground ☐

tree ☐

air ☐

bush ☐

feeder ☐

other:

NOTES

BIRD'S SKETCH

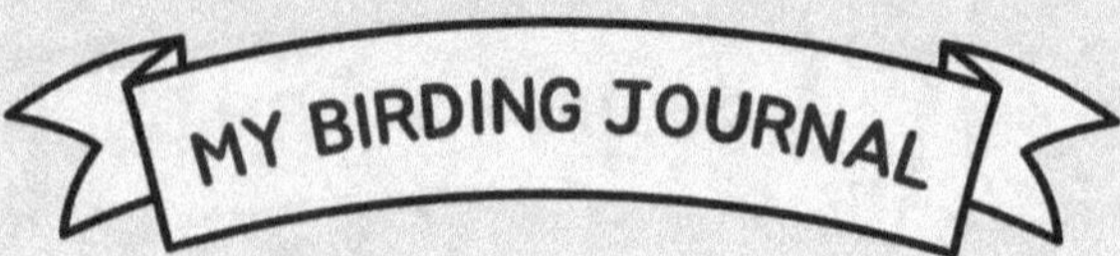

DATE:

SEASON:

WEATHER:

TIME:

HABITAT:

TEMPERATURE:

LOCATION:

BIRD'S NAME:

NESTING:

COLOR AND MARKINGS:

BIRD'S BEHAVIOR:

MALE/FEMALE/NOT SURE

NUMBER OF BIRDS OBSERVED:

BIRD LOCATION

ground ☐

tree ☐

air ☐

bush ☐

feeder ☐

other:

NOTES

BIRD'S SKETCH

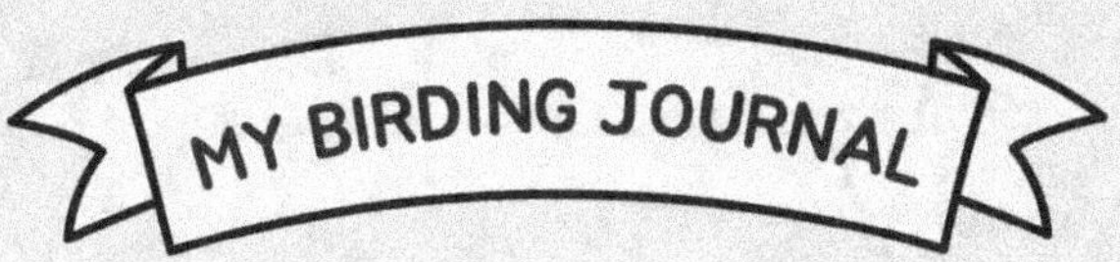

DATE:

SEASON:

WEATHER:

TIME:

HABITAT:

TEMPERATURE:

LOCATION:

BIRD'S NAME:	NESTING:
COLOR AND MARKINGS:	BIRD'S BEHAVIOR:
MALE/FEMALE/NOT SURE	NUMBER OF BIRDS OBSERVED:

BIRD LOCATION

ground ☐

tree ☐

air ☐

bush ☐

feeder ☐

other:

NOTES

BIRD'S SKETCH

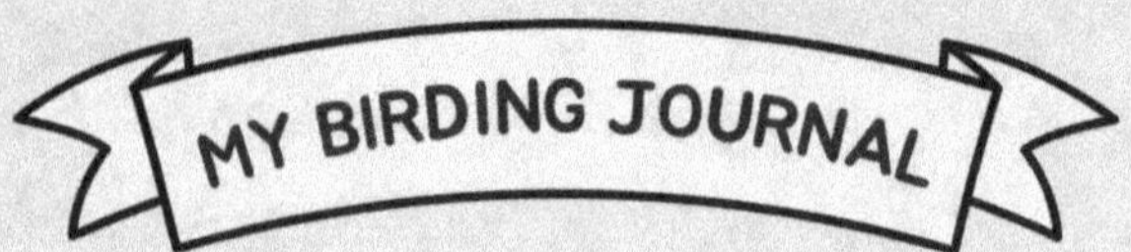

DATE:

SEASON:

WEATHER:

TIME:

HABITAT:

TEMPERATURE:

LOCATION:

BIRD'S NAME:

NESTING:

COLOR AND MARKINGS:

BIRD'S BEHAVIOR:

MALE/FEMALE/NOT SURE

NUMBER OF BIRDS OBSERVED:

BIRD LOCATION

ground ☐
tree ☐
air ☐
bush ☐
feeder ☐
other:

NOTES

BIRD'S SKETCH

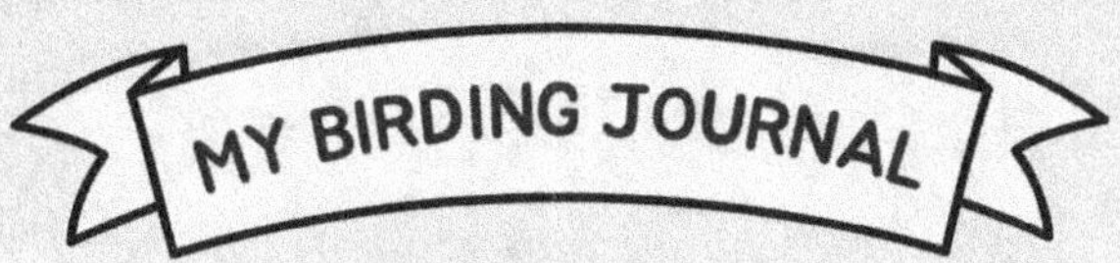

DATE:

SEASON:

WEATHER:

TIME:

HABITAT:

TEMPERATURE:

LOCATION:

BIRD'S NAME:	NESTING:
COLOR AND MARKINGS:	BIRD'S BEHAVIOR:
MALE/FEMALE/NOT SURE	NUMBER OF BIRDS OBSERVED:

BIRD LOCATION

ground ☐

tree ☐

air ☐

bush ☐

feeder ☐

other:

NOTES

BIRD'S SKETCH

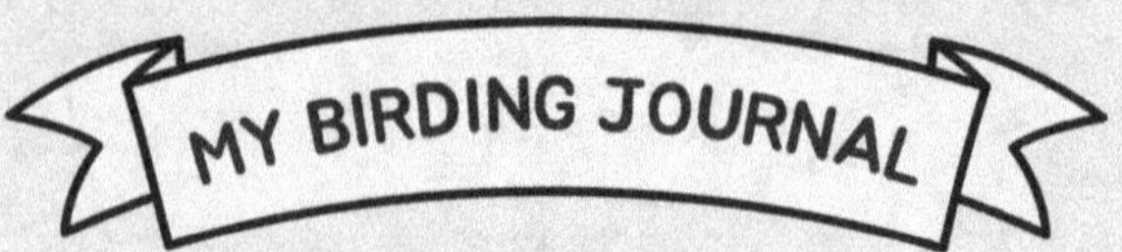

DATE:

SEASON:

WEATHER:

TIME:

HABITAT:

TEMPERATURE:

LOCATION:

BIRD'S NAME:	NESTING:
COLOR AND MARKINGS:	BIRD'S BEHAVIOR:
MALE/FEMALE/NOT SURE	NUMBER OF BIRDS OBSERVED:

BIRD LOCATION

ground ☐

tree ☐

air ☐

bush ☐

feeder ☐

other:

NOTES

BIRD'S SKETCH

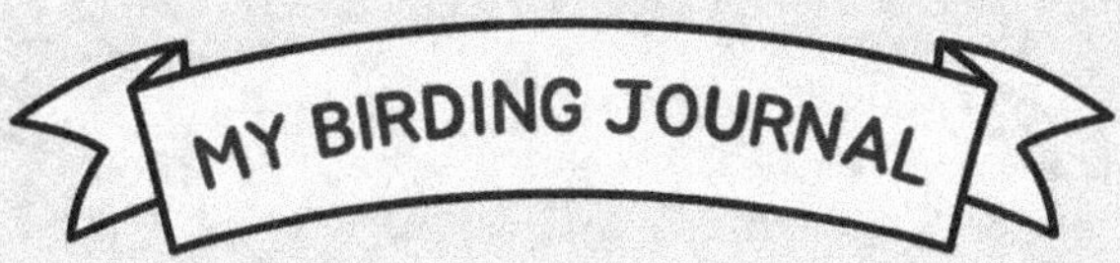

DATE:

SEASON:

WEATHER:

TIME:

HABITAT:

TEMPERATURE:

LOCATION:

BIRD'S NAME:

NESTING:

COLOR AND MARKINGS:

BIRD'S BEHAVIOR:

MALE/FEMALE/NOT SURE

NUMBER OF BIRDS OBSERVED:

BIRD LOCATION

ground

tree

air

bush

feeder

other:

NOTES

BIRD'S SKETCH

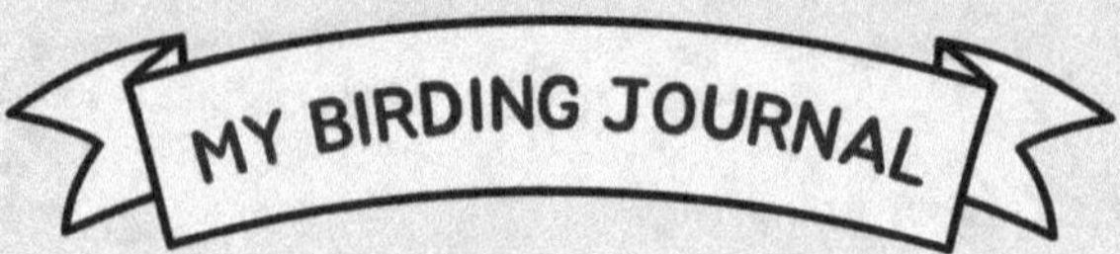

DATE:

SEASON:

WEATHER:

TIME:

HABITAT:

TEMPERATURE:

LOCATION:

BIRD'S NAME:

NESTING:

COLOR AND MARKINGS:

BIRD'S BEHAVIOR:

MALE/FEMALE/NOT SURE

NUMBER OF BIRDS OBSERVED:

BIRD LOCATION

ground ☐
tree ☐
air ☐
bush ☐
feeder ☐
other:

NOTES

BIRD'S SKETCH

DATE:

SEASON:

WEATHER:

TIME:

HABITAT:

TEMPERATURE:

LOCATION:

BIRD'S NAME:	NESTING:
COLOR AND MARKINGS:	BIRD'S BEHAVIOR:
MALE/FEMALE/NOT SURE	NUMBER OF BIRDS OBSERVED:

BIRD LOCATION

ground ☐

tree ☐

air ☐

bush ☐

feeder ☐

other:

NOTES

BIRD'S SKETCH

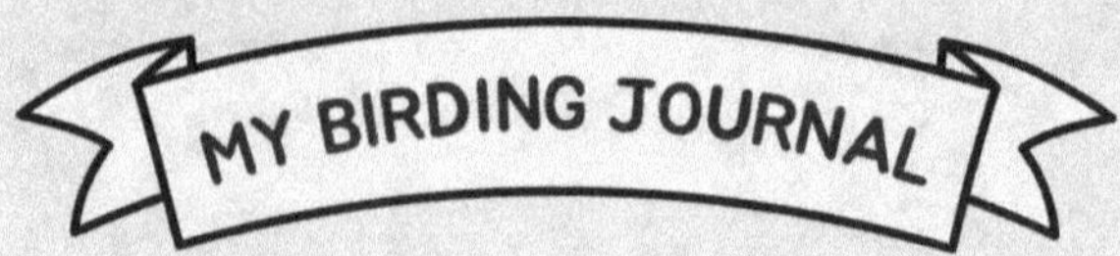

DATE:

SEASON:

WEATHER:

TIME:

HABITAT:

TEMPERATURE:

LOCATION:

BIRD'S NAME:	NESTING:
COLOR AND MARKINGS:	BIRD'S BEHAVIOR:
MALE/FEMALE/NOT SURE	NUMBER OF BIRDS OBSERVED:

BIRD LOCATION

ground ☐

tree ☐

air ☐

bush ☐

feeder ☐

other:

NOTES

BIRD'S SKETCH

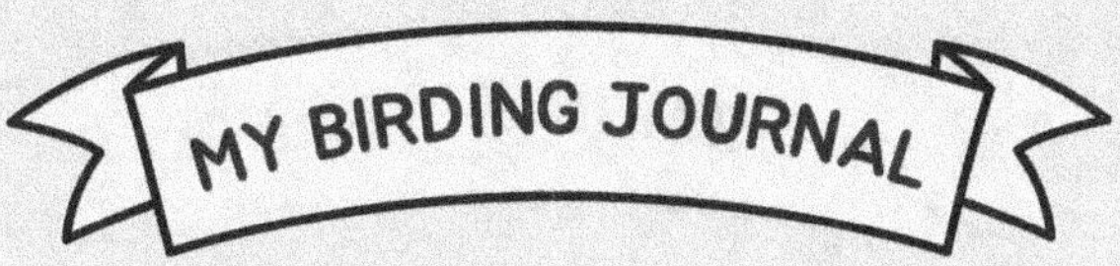

DATE:

SEASON:

WEATHER:

TIME:

HABITAT:

TEMPERATURE:

LOCATION:

BIRD'S NAME:	NESTING:
COLOR AND MARKINGS:	BIRD'S BEHAVIOR:
MALE/FEMALE/NOT SURE	NUMBER OF BIRDS OBSERVED:

BIRD LOCATION

ground ☐

tree ☐

air ☐

bush ☐

feeder ☐

other:

NOTES

BIRD'S SKETCH

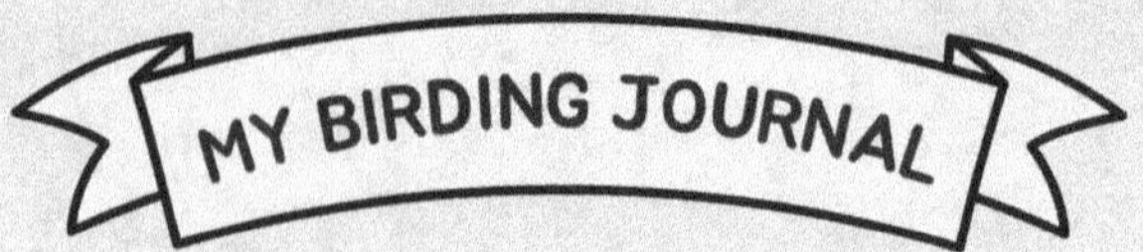

DATE:

SEASON:

WEATHER:

TIME:

HABITAT:

TEMPERATURE:

LOCATION:

BIRD'S NAME:

NESTING:

COLOR AND MARKINGS:

BIRD'S BEHAVIOR:

MALE/FEMALE/NOT SURE

NUMBER OF BIRDS OBSERVED:

BIRD LOCATION

ground ☐

tree ☐

air ☐

bush ☐

feeder ☐

other:

NOTES

BIRD'S SKETCH

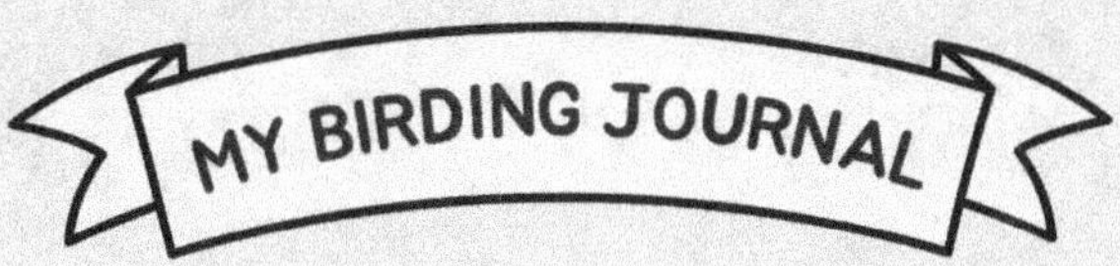

DATE:

SEASON:

WEATHER:

TIME:

HABITAT:

TEMPERATURE:

LOCATION:

BIRD'S NAME:

NESTING:

COLOR AND MARKINGS:

BIRD'S BEHAVIOR:

MALE/FEMALE/NOT SURE

NUMBER OF BIRDS OBSERVED:

BIRD LOCATION

ground ☐

tree ☐

air ☐

bush ☐

feeder ☐

other:

NOTES

BIRD'S SKETCH

DATE:

SEASON:

TIME:

HABITAT:

WEATHER:

TEMPERATURE:

LOCATION:

BIRD'S NAME:

NESTING:

COLOR AND MARKINGS:

BIRD'S BEHAVIOR:

MALE/FEMALE/NOT SURE

NUMBER OF BIRDS OBSERVED:

BIRD LOCATION

ground ☐

tree ☐

air ☐

bush ☐

feeder ☐

other:

NOTES

BIRD'S SKETCH

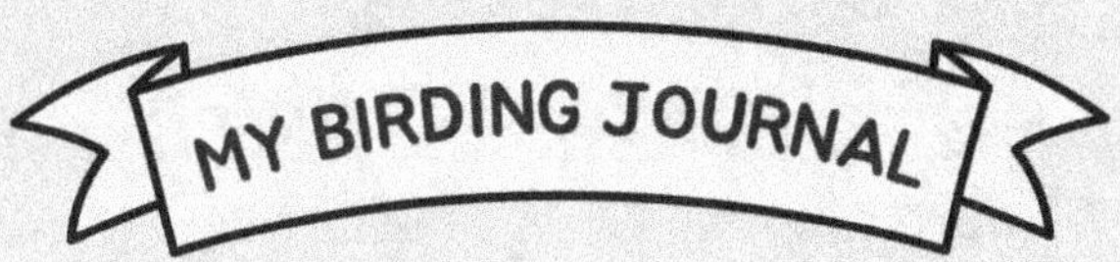

DATE:

SEASON:

WEATHER:

TIME:

HABITAT:

TEMPERATURE:

LOCATION:

BIRD'S NAME:	NESTING:
COLOR AND MARKINGS:	BIRD'S BEHAVIOR:
MALE/FEMALE/NOT SURE	NUMBER OF BIRDS OBSERVED:

BIRD LOCATION

ground ☐
tree ☐
air ☐
bush ☐
feeder ☐
other:

NOTES

BIRD'S SKETCH

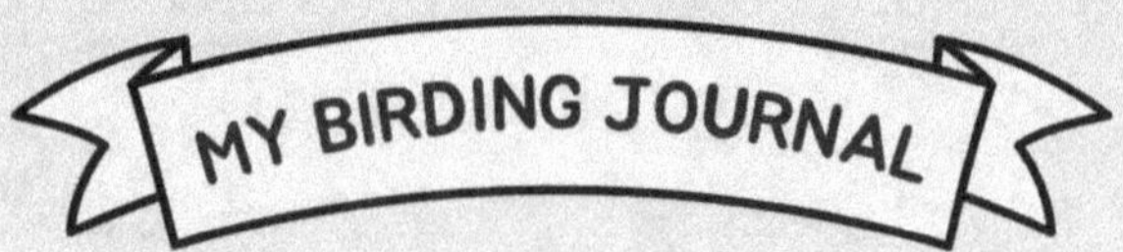

DATE:

SEASON:

WEATHER:

TIME:

HABITAT:

TEMPERATURE:

LOCATION:

BIRD'S NAME:

NESTING:

COLOR AND MARKINGS:

BIRD'S BEHAVIOR:

MALE/FEMALE/NOT SURE

NUMBER OF BIRDS OBSERVED:

BIRD LOCATION

ground ☐

tree ☐

air ☐

bush ☐

feeder ☐

other:

NOTES

BIRD'S SKETCH

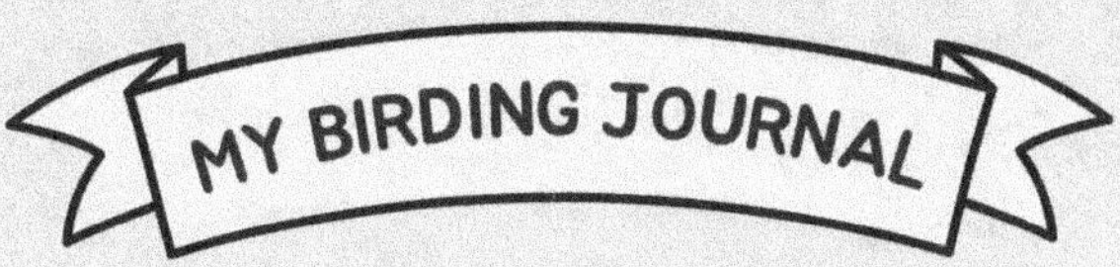

DATE:

SEASON:

WEATHER:

TIME:

HABITAT:

TEMPERATURE:

LOCATION:

BIRD'S NAME:	NESTING:
COLOR AND MARKINGS:	BIRD'S BEHAVIOR:
MALE/FEMALE/NOT SURE	NUMBER OF BIRDS OBSERVED:

BIRD LOCATION

ground ☐

tree ☐

air ☐

bush ☐

feeder ☐

other:

NOTES

BIRD'S SKETCH

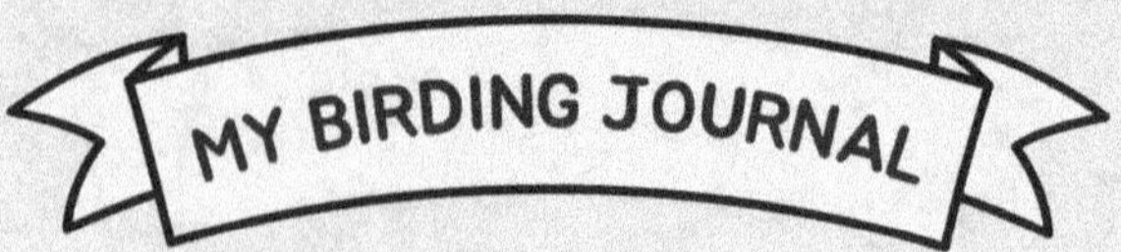

DATE:

SEASON:

WEATHER:

TIME:

HABITAT:

TEMPERATURE:

LOCATION:

BIRD'S NAME:

NESTING:

COLOR AND MARKINGS:

BIRD'S BEHAVIOR:

MALE/FEMALE/NOT SURE

NUMBER OF BIRDS OBSERVED:

BIRD LOCATION

ground ☐

tree ☐

air ☐

bush ☐

feeder ☐

other:

NOTES

BIRD'S SKETCH

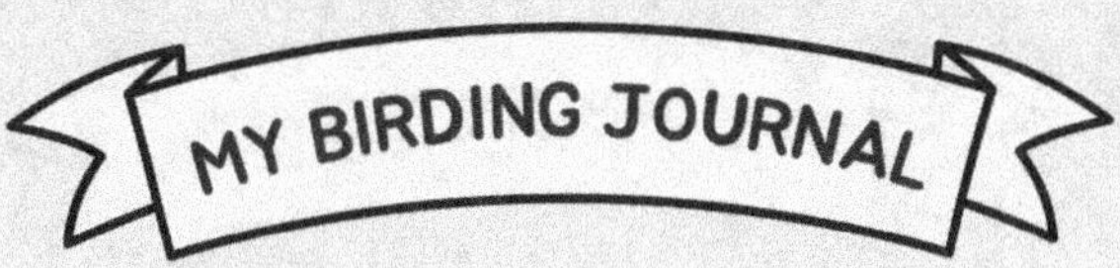

DATE:

SEASON:

WEATHER:

TIME:

HABITAT:

TEMPERATURE:

LOCATION:

BIRD'S NAME:

NESTING:

COLOR AND MARKINGS:

BIRD'S BEHAVIOR:

MALE/FEMALE/NOT SURE

NUMBER OF BIRDS OBSERVED:

BIRD LOCATION

ground

tree

air

bush

feeder

other:

NOTES

BIRD'S SKETCH

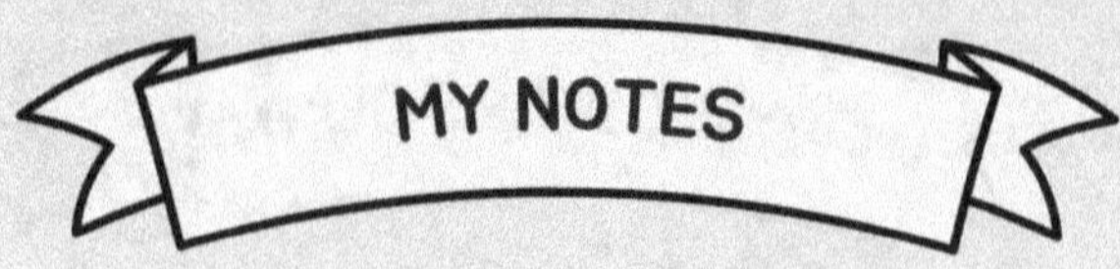

Notes on any other wildlife or interesting observations made during the birdwatching trip, such as insects, mammals, etc.

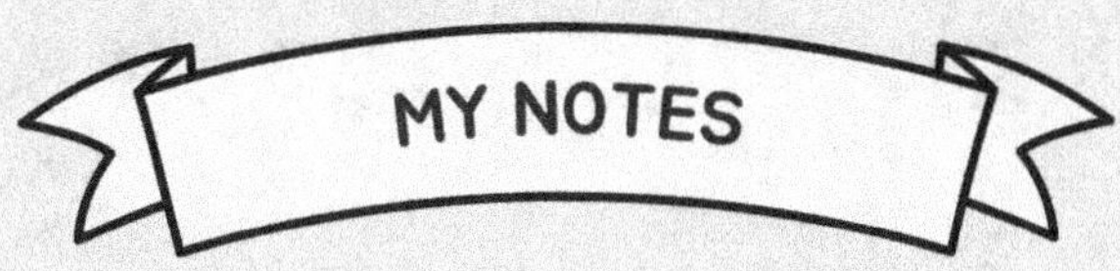

Notes on any other wildlife or interesting observations made during the birdwatching trip, such as insects, mammals, etc.

UNUSUAL OR INTERESTING BEHAVIORS

NOTES FOR MY NEXT TRIP

UNUSUAL OR INTERESTING BEHAVIORS

NOTES FOR MY NEXT TRIP

MY SKETCHES

BIRD FEATHERS THAT I FOUND

BIRD FOOTPRINT THAT I OBSERVED

BIRD FEATHERS THAT I FOUND

BIRD FOOTPRINT THAT I OBSERVED

Bird Name	When	Bird's Location	Bird's Behavior	Comments

Bird Name	When	Bird's Location	Bird's Behavior	Comments

Bird Name	When	Bird's Location	Bird's Behavior	Comments

Bird Name	When	Bird's Location	Bird's Behavior	Comments

let's do people-watching

Tweet: Hey, Chirp, have you ever heard of "people-watching"? It's like bird watching, but for humans!
Chirp: Humans? Why would anyone want to watch them? They don't have feathers!
Tweet: Well, some humans have funny hats and bright clothes. It can be pretty entertaining!
Chirp: Hmm, I'm not convinced. What's the point?
Tweet: The point is to observe and appreciate the humans in their natural habitat, just like we appreciate birds in the wild!
Chirp: I suppose that makes sense. So where should we go for this people-watching trip?
Tweet: How about the park? There's always a lot of humans there doing weird things.
Chirp: Great idea! But how do we prepare for people-watching?
Tweet: Well, we can bring some popcorn and a pair of binoculars. And maybe a notebook to write down all the funny things we see!
Chirp: Oh boy, this is going to be hilarious! Let's do it!
Tweet: Okay, but remember, we have to be stealthy. We don't want the humans to notice us watching them!
Chirp: Right, right. I'll be like a ninja bird, sneaking around unnoticed.
Tweet: (laughing) Okay, ninja bird.
Let's go people-watching!

LOVEBIRD MAZE

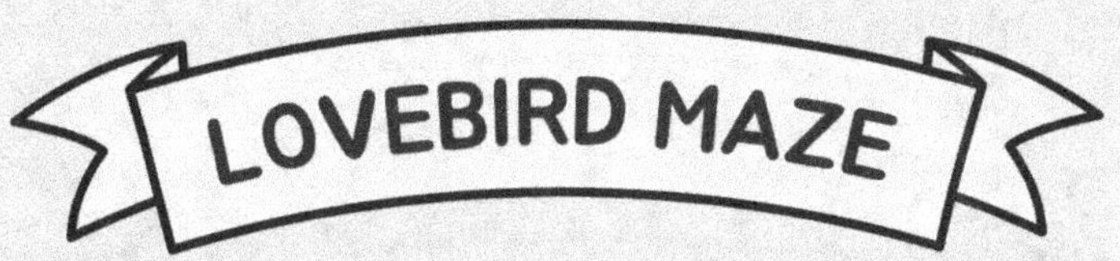

Help the lovebird find its way to its mate at the center of the heart. Navigate through twists and turns, avoiding dead ends and obstacles along the way. Can you guide the lovebird to a happy reunion with its sweetheart?

Good luck!

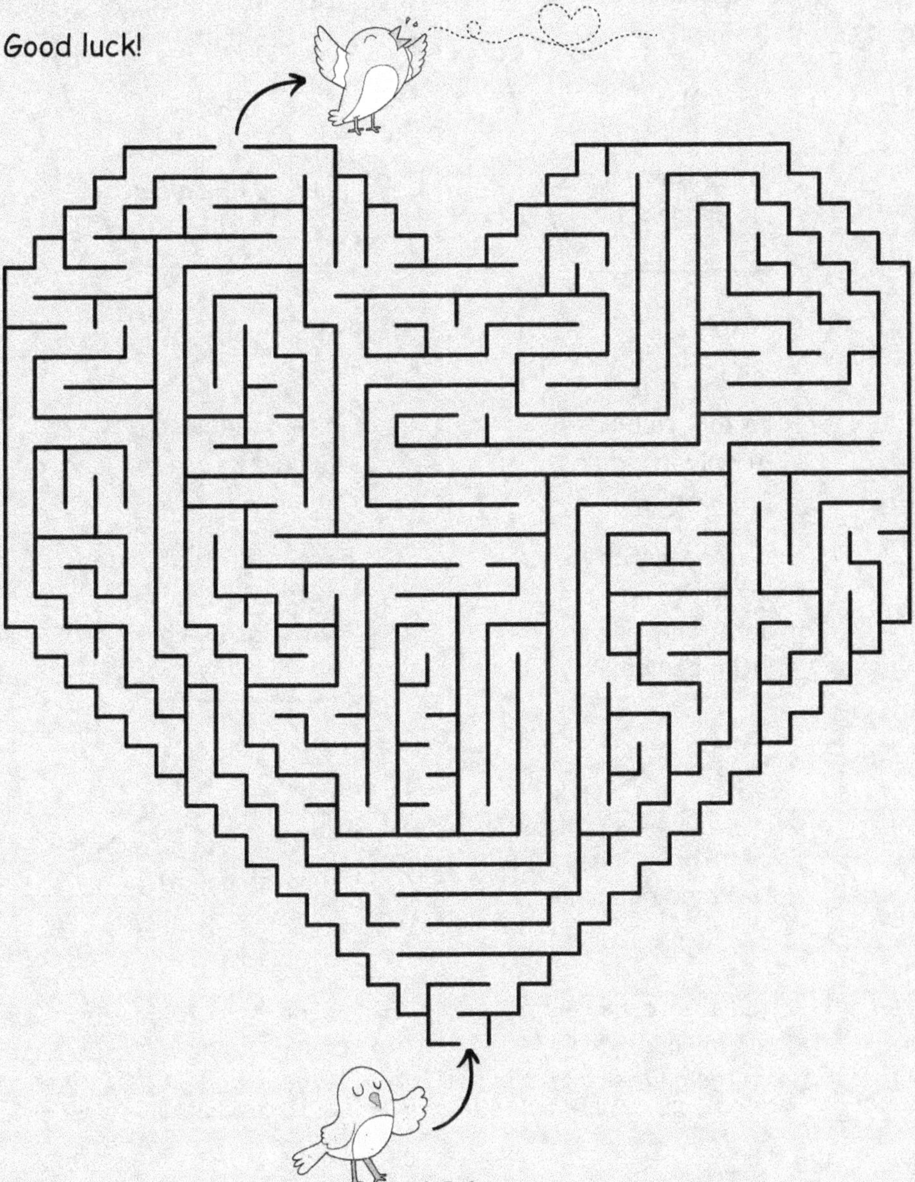

have
wings made of
pizza

OR

have feathers made
of spaghetti?

have a
beak that shoots
confetti

OR

have feathers that
light up like a disco
ball?

be able
to talk to birds
but only in riddles

OR

have the power to
shape-shift into any
bird but only for one
hour per day?

have the
power to lay eggs
whenever you want

OR

have a tail that can
extend and grab
things like a
monkey?

have a
voice that sounds
like a bird chirping

OR

a tail that can grow
and shrink like a
slinky?

have a
nest made of
marshmallows

OR

feathers that
change color with
your mood?

Bird Species Word Search Challenge

N	I	B	O	R	N	A	C	I	R	E	M	A	A
O	E	R	I	V	U	S	T	A	R	L	I	N	G
C	C	W	T	S	W	B	L	U	E	B	I	R	D
C	A	R	D	I	N	A	L	R	R	M	A	H	I
A	D	R	I	B	G	N	I	M	M	U	H	A	I
T	L	O	O	W	N	U	T	H	A	T	C	H	H
D	G	R	R	W	A	R	B	L	E	R	C	H	W
G	I	R	R	C	T	I	T	M	O	U	S	E	O
N	R	K	A	C	H	I	C	K	A	D	E	E	R
O	E	L	S	C	D	C	A	T	B	I	R	D	R
E	A	E	I	C	K	N	B	A	C	L	E	O	A
G	Y	A	J	E	U	L	B	C	A	R	N	A	P
I	J	U	N	C	O	N	E	I	U	H	O	L	S
P	T	B	A	R	N	S	W	A	L	L	O	W	C

American Robin	Crow	Barn Swallow
Cardinal	Sparrow	Hummingbird
Catbird	Vireo	Titmouse
Blue Jay	Grackle	Warbler
Pigeon	Junco	Bluebird
Starling	Nuthatch	Chickadee

Playing "Bird Bingo" is simple and fun! To play the game, all you need to do is keep an eye out for the birds as you go about your bird-watching adventures. Whenever you spot a bird that matches one of the birds on the page, mark off that square. The goal is to mark off as many squares as possible, and once you have marked off five squares in a row (horizontally, vertically, or diagonally), shout out "Bingo!" and congratulate yourself on your bird-watching skills!

Have fun and happy bird-watching!

BINGO!	American Robin	Yellow-rumped Warbler	Downy Woodpecker
Barn Swallow	European Starling	Anna's Hummingbird	Northern Flicker
American Goldfinch	Black-capped Chickadee	American Crow	Baltimore Oriole
Dark-eyed Junco	Blue Jay	House Finch	Common Grackle

save that woman!

Tweet: (whispering) Look over there! That human is trying to ride a bike, but they keep falling off!

Chirp: (also whispering) Ha! They look so silly! Why would anyone want to ride on two wheels?

Tweet: (chuckles) Who knows? But it's funny to watch them try!

Chirp: (excitedly) Oh, look! That human is walking a small furry creature on a leash. Do you think it's a dog?

Tweet: (also excitedly) It must be! And look at the way it's wagging its tail. Humans and their dogs are so adorable!

Chirp: (whispering) Look over there! That human is running so fast! Do you think they're running away from something?

Tweet: (also whispering) Maybe they're running away from a predator. Humans are pretty slow, they're easy targets for other creatures.

Chirp: (concerned) Oh no, we have to help her! We can't let her get eaten!

Tweet: (nodding) You're right, let's fly closer and see if we can scare off whatever is chasing her.

(Birds fly closer to the woman and see that she's wearing running shoes and headphones.)

Chirp: (confused) Wait a minute, she's not running away from anything! She's just running for fun!

Tweet: (surprised) Really? Why would anyone run for fun?

Chirp: (shrugs) I have no idea. Humans are so weird.

Tweet: (shrugs) Humans are full of mysteries.

Chirp: (giggles) And full of funny things to watch! Let's keep people-watching, this is too much fun!

Can you find all these bird behaviors while out birdwatching?

Use the checklist to mark off the behaviors you see, and don't forget to write down the bird species you observe. To make it even more fun, try to find all the behaviors in one outing or challenge yourself to find new behaviors on each birdwatching trip.

Happy birding!

- ☐ Flying in a flock _______________________
- ☐ Nest building _______________________
- ☐ Bathing _______________________
- ☐ Singing or Calling _______________________
- ☐ Feeding _______________________
- ☐ Preening _______________________
- ☐ Sunbathing _______________________
- ☐ Mating dance _______________________
- ☐ Flying solo _______________________
- ☐ Perching _______________________
- ☐ Foraging _______________________
- ☐ Other: _______________________

Bird Watching Word Search Challenge

A	F	T	I	R	R	S	O	N	G	B	I	R	D
S	T	T	S	E	N	A	A	T	A	E	W	H	T
H	H	S	L	A	E	B	P	R	N	G	I	I	E
O	I	I	I	O	C	O	I	T	R	I	N	B	O
R	R	U	L	A	E	H	B	N	O	E	G	R	T
E	B	P	E	R	C	H	I	N	G	R	S	E	S
B	I	N	O	C	U	L	A	R	S	I	E	C	H
I	D	E	E	S	D	R	I	B	P	W	A	O	E
R	K	C	O	L	F	F	E	A	T	H	E	R	S
D	R	A	U	E	N	C	H	A	B	I	T	A	T
T	H	G	I	L	F	D	B	H	K	B	M	T	C
N	R	A	B	M	I	G	R	A	T	I	O	N	D
E	C	H	I	C	K	S	E	I	L	B	T	S	F
D	D	B	A	K	C	B	P	L	U	M	A	G	E

binoculars	songbird	feathers
chirp	chicks	tweet
wings	flight	birdseed
nest	habitat	plumage
flock	perching	beak
migration	raptor	shorebird

Why did the chicken cross the playground? To get to the other slide!

Why do seagulls fly over the sea? Because if they flew over the bay, they'd be bagels!

How do you know if a bird is bald? When you see its feathers falling out!

What do you call a bird that's afraid to fly? A chicken!

Why do hummingbirds hum? Because they don't know the words!

Why don't penguins like talking to strangers at parties? They're too shy to break the ice!

What do you get when you cross a bird and a pig? A bird that oinks!

Why did the owl invite his friends over? He didn't want to be owl by himself!

BIRD TREE MAZE

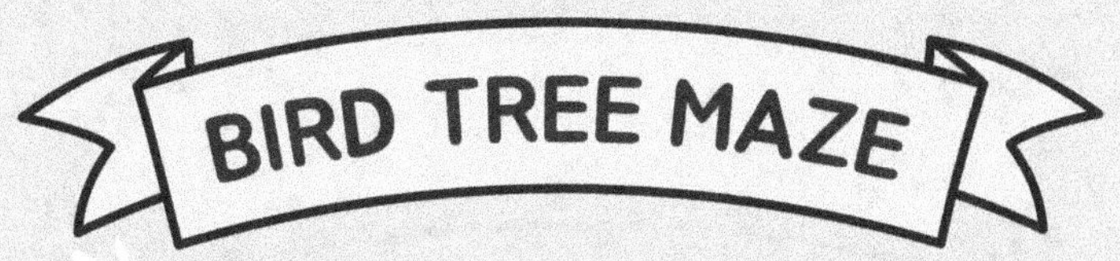

Your goal is to help the bird reach the top of the tree to meet its friend. Navigate the maze by finding the correct path, avoiding dead ends, and using your bird-watching skills to spot clues along the way.

You might encounter some obstacles, but don't give up! Keep flapping those wings and you'll reach the top in no time.

Good luck!

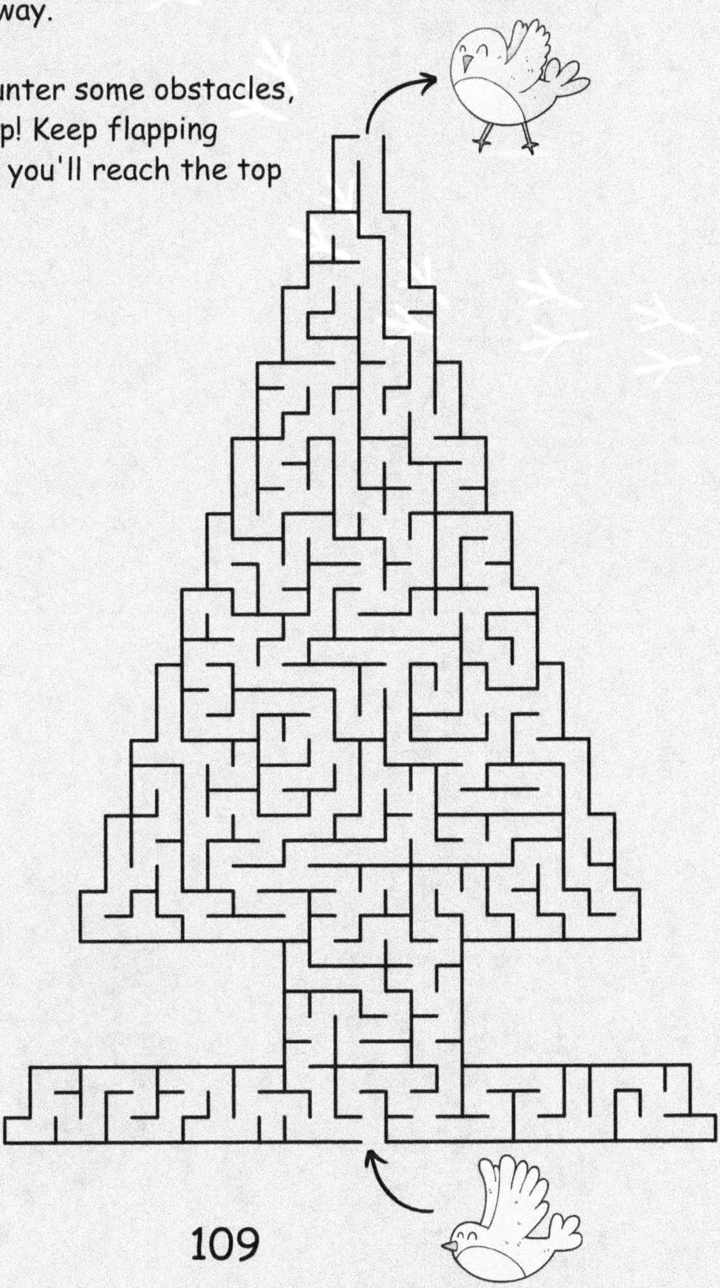

HOW TO DRAW A SWALLOW

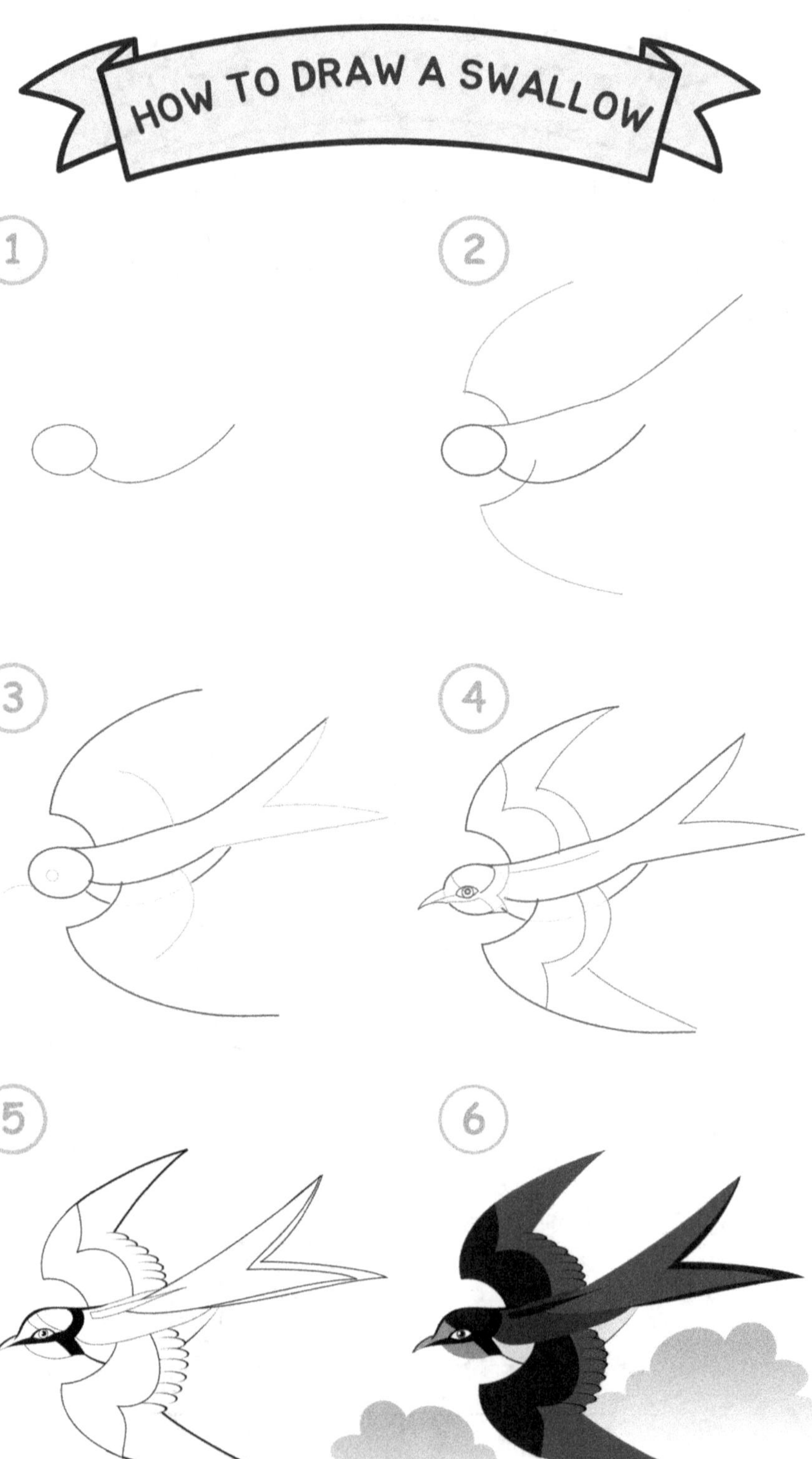

HOW TO DRAW A HOOPOE

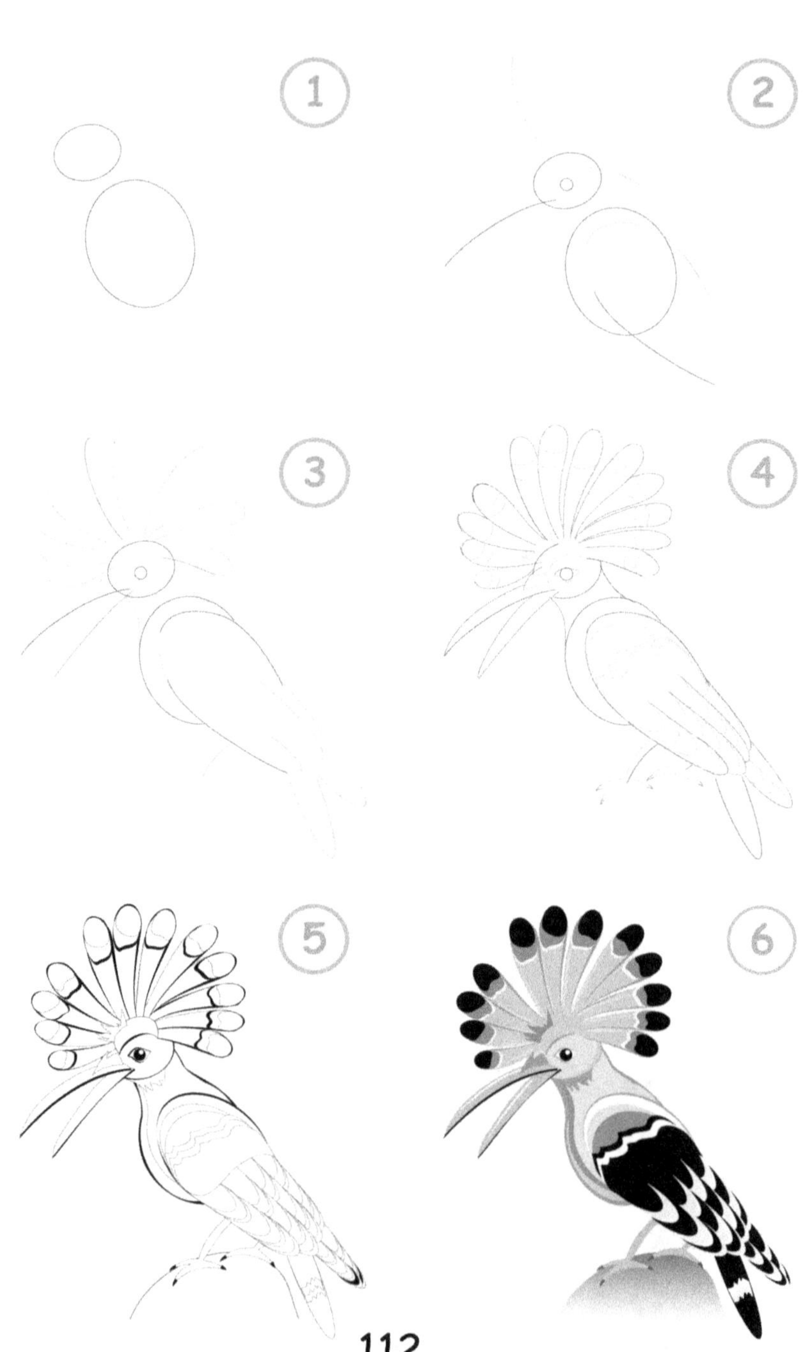

a bestseller is born

Tweet: (laughing) I think we've seen enough humans for one day. My wings are tired from all this flying!

Chirp: (also laughing) Yeah, but we have to admit, humans are pretty funny creatures.

Tweet: (nodding) Definitely. Did you see the way that one was walking? It was like they had something stuck in their foot!

Chirp: (chuckles) Or the way that other one was talking to themselves? Humans are always doing strange things.

Tweet: (thinks for a moment) You know, we might be onto something here. Maybe we could write a book about our people-watching adventures!

Chirp: (excitedly) Yes! We could call it "The Secret Life of Humans", and it could be a bestseller!

Tweet: (smiling) Or "Humans: A Field Guide for Birds". We could include all our observations and funny conclusions.

Chirp: (nodding) I like it! And who knows, maybe we could even teach other birds how to people-watch!

Tweet: (laughing) We'll have to start a whole new trend! People-watching will become the next big thing in the bird world!

Chirp: (grinning) And we'll be the pioneers of it all! The bird world will never be the same.

American Robin

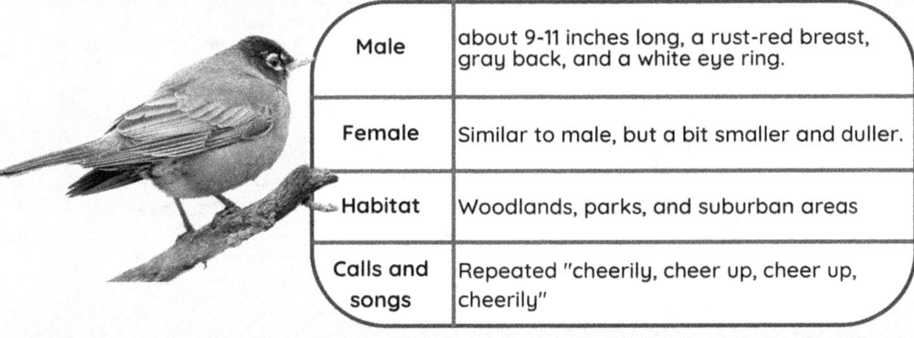

Male	about 9-11 inches long, a rust-red breast, gray back, and a white eye ring.
Female	Similar to male, but a bit smaller and duller.
Habitat	Woodlands, parks, and suburban areas
Calls and songs	Repeated "cheerily, cheer up, cheer up, cheerily"

House Sparrow

Male	Gray crown and cheeks, black bib
Female	Brownish-gray feathers
Habitat	Cities and towns, farms, and fields
Calls and songs	Chirps and tweets

American Goldfinch

Male	Bright yellow body, black wings
Female	Duller yellow body, black wings
Habitat	Fields, meadows, and gardens
Calls and songs	Sweet, twittering song

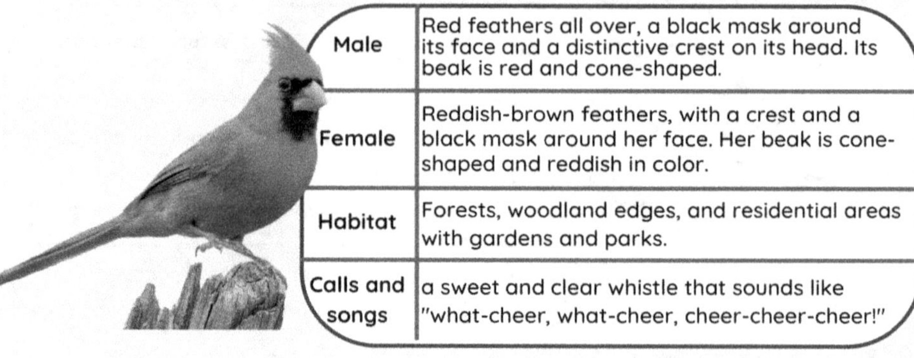

Male	Red feathers all over, a black mask around its face and a distinctive crest on its head. Its beak is red and cone-shaped.
Female	Reddish-brown feathers, with a crest and a black mask around her face. Her beak is cone-shaped and reddish in color.
Habitat	Forests, woodland edges, and residential areas with gardens and parks.
Calls and songs	a sweet and clear whistle that sounds like "what-cheer, what-cheer, cheer-cheer-cheer!"

Blue Jay

Male	Blue feathers on their wings, tail, and head, with a white and black pattern on their face and a grayish-brown back.
Female	A bit more muted than the male, with a blue-gray head, back, and wings, a pale gray underbelly, and a blue-tipped tail.
Habitat	Deciduous and mixed forests, parks, and residential areas.
Calls and songs	High-pitched sounds, as whistles, squawks, and rattles. A loud "jay-jay" call and a quieter, more melodious "queedle-queedle" call.

Baltimore Oriole

Male	Orange plumage on their body and black on their wings and head. A black throat and a small white patch on the wings.
Female	Olive-yellow and brownish feathers, with black markings on the wings and tail. A brighter yellow underside than the male.
Habitat	Woodlands, parks, and suburban areas
Calls and songs	Their singing is a series of whistled notes that sound like "wheeee, wheeeo, wheee, wheeeo". Their call is a harsh, chattering "chck, chck, chck".

Barn Swallow

Male	Dark blue back and wings, rusty-red throat and forehead, long forked tail. They are small and agile with a streamlined body.
Female	Lighter blue back and wings, buff-colored throat and forehead, shorter forked tail. They are smaller than males.
Habitat	Open habitats near water, such as barns, bridges, and cliffs.
Calls and songs	a beautiful, musical chirp that sounds like a cheerful "chee-weet" or "tseep-tseep".

European Starling

Male	Metallic green and purple plumage with white spots in winter, and a sharp, pointed bill. Medium-sized with a stocky build.
Female	Duller brown plumage with white spots in winter, and a shorter, less pointed bill. Slightly smaller than males.
Habitat	Open habitats, including fields, lawns, and urban areas.
Calls and songs	Whistles, trills, and warbles, as well as mimicking other bird calls and human speech.

Mourning Dove

Male	Brownish-gray with a pinkish hue, a small head, and a long, pointed tail. Medium-sized with a plump body.
Female	Similar to males, but slightly smaller and with less iridescence.
Habitat	open habitats, including fields, parks, and residential areas.
Calls and songs	A mournful cooing sound that sounds like "who-oo-oo."

American Crow

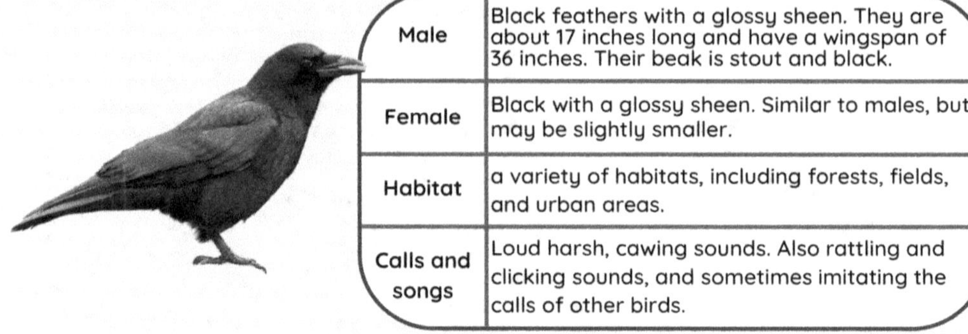

Male	Black feathers with a glossy sheen. They are about 17 inches long and have a wingspan of 36 inches. Their beak is stout and black.
Female	Black with a glossy sheen. Similar to males, but may be slightly smaller.
Habitat	a variety of habitats, including forests, fields, and urban areas.
Calls and songs	Loud harsh, cawing sounds. Also rattling and clicking sounds, and sometimes imitating the calls of other birds.

Song Sparrow

Male	A brown back with dark streaks, a white or gray breast with brown streaks, and a brown cap. About 6.5 inches long.
Female	Similar to males, but slightly duller in color. About 6.5 inches long.
Habitat	fields, meadows, and suburban areas.
Calls and songs	a complex and melodious song, consisting of several short phrases repeated in a distinct pattern. Also a sharp "tik" and a trill.

Red-Winged Blackbird

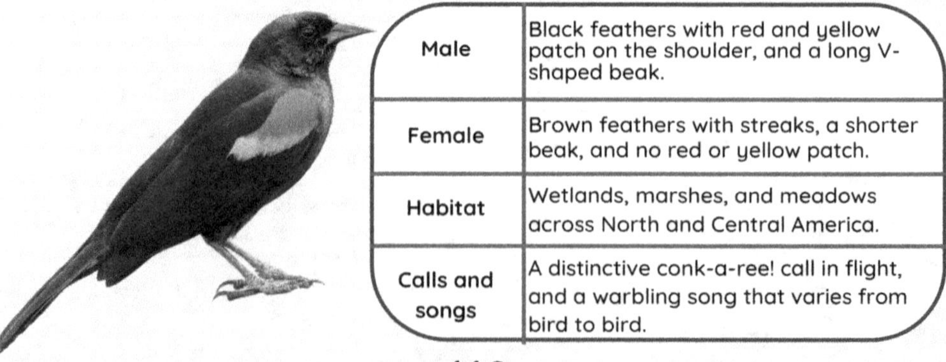

Male	Black feathers with red and yellow patch on the shoulder, and a long V-shaped beak.
Female	Brown feathers with streaks, a shorter beak, and no red or yellow patch.
Habitat	Wetlands, marshes, and meadows across North and Central America.
Calls and songs	A distinctive conk-a-ree! call in flight, and a warbling song that varies from bird to bird.

House Finch

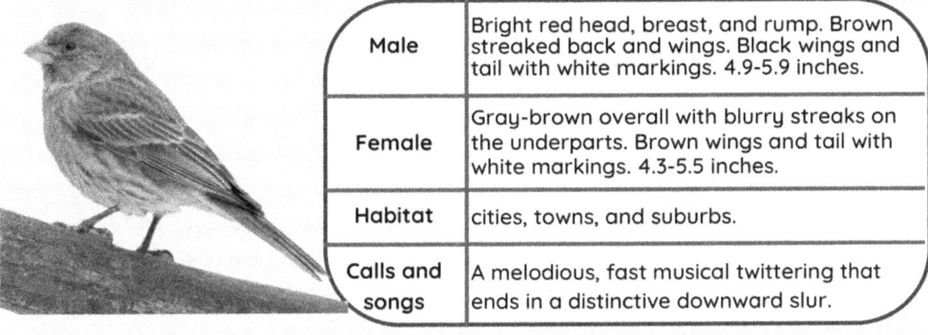

Male	Bright red head, breast, and rump. Brown streaked back and wings. Black wings and tail with white markings. 4.9-5.9 inches.
Female	Gray-brown overall with blurry streaks on the underparts. Brown wings and tail with white markings. 4.3-5.5 inches.
Habitat	cities, towns, and suburbs.
Calls and songs	A melodious, fast musical twittering that ends in a distinctive downward slur.

Downy Woodpecker

Male	Black and white with red spot on head. Small in size, 5.5 - 6.7 inches.
Female	Lack and white with red spot on head. Small in size, 5.5 - 6.7 inches.
Habitat	Forests, woodlands, and suburban
Calls and songs	High-pitched pik and rapid drumming sounds.

Red-bellied Woodpecker

Male	Red cap and nape, white and black striped face, gray-brown back and wings, light-colored belly with a faint red tint. 9-10.6 inches. Long, pointed bill.
Female	Similar to males, but with a slightly smaller and less vivid red cap. 8.5-9.4 inches.
Habitat	Woodlands, forest edges, suburban parks, and gardens.
Calls and songs	A rolling "churr" sound, sometimes followed by a "pik" or "tchik" call.

Black-capped Chickadee

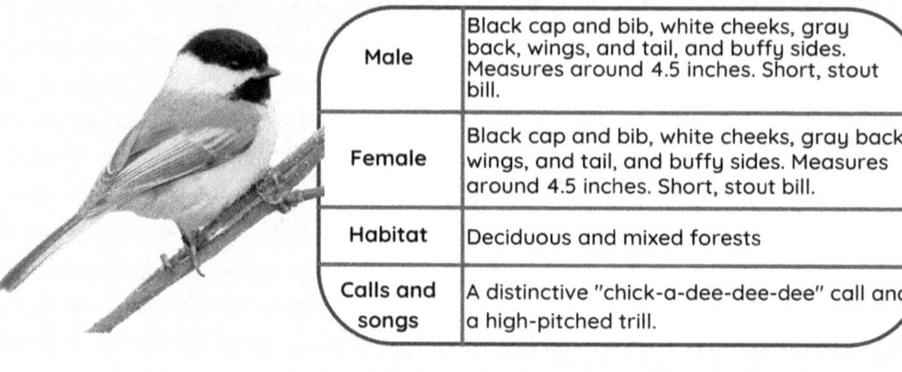

Male	Black cap and bib, white cheeks, gray back, wings, and tail, and buffy sides. Measures around 4.5 inches. Short, stout bill.
Female	Black cap and bib, white cheeks, gray back, wings, and tail, and buffy sides. Measures around 4.5 inches. Short, stout bill.
Habitat	Deciduous and mixed forests
Calls and songs	A distinctive "chick-a-dee-dee-dee" call and a high-pitched trill.

Tufted Titmouse

Male	Blue-gray back and white belly with a distinctive crest on head. Small in size 4.5 - 6.5 inches.
Female	Gray back and white belly with a distinctive crest on head. Small in size 4.5 - 6.5 inches.
Habitat	Deciduous forests and woodlands.
Calls and songs	A whistled "peter-peter-peter" or "peter-peter," sometimes with a series of clear whistles.

Dark-eyed Junco

Male	Dark gray head and back with white belly and pinkish-brown sides. Small in size 5.5 - 6.3 inches.
Female	Brown head and back with white belly and pinkish-brown sides. Small in size 5.5 - 6.3 inches.
Habitat	Forests, fields, and gardens
Calls and songs	Musical trill and a "tick" call note.

White-breasted Nuthatch

Male	Blue-gray back, white underparts, black cap and eye stripe. Around 5.5 inches. Short, straight bill and strong legs.
Female	Blue-gray back, white underparts, black cap and eye stripe. Around 5.5 inches. Short, straight bill and strong legs.
Habitat	deciduous forests, mixed forests, and suburban areas.
Calls and songs	a nasal "yank yank" call and a series of high-pitched notes.

Northern Flicker

Male	Black mustache stripe, a red crescent on the nape of the neck, and black spots on the underside of the wings. Around 12 inches. Long, slightly curved bill.
Female	Black mustache stripe and a red spot on the nape of the neck. Measures around 12 inches. Long, slightly curved bill.
Habitat	Open habitats with trees, such as forests, woodlands, and suburban areas.
Calls and songs	a loud, rhythmic "wicka wicka" call and a series of high-pitched notes.

Carolina Wren

Male	Rusty-brown back, warm-brown underparts, white eyebrow stripe, and a long, curved beak. Around 5.5 inches.
Female	Rusty-brown back, warm-brown underparts, white eyebrow stripe, and a long, curved beak. Around 5.5 inches.
Habitat	Wooded areas, gardens, and parks
Calls and songs	a loud, cheerful "tea-kettle, tea-kettle, tea-kettle" song and a series of high-pitched notes.

Northern Mockingbird

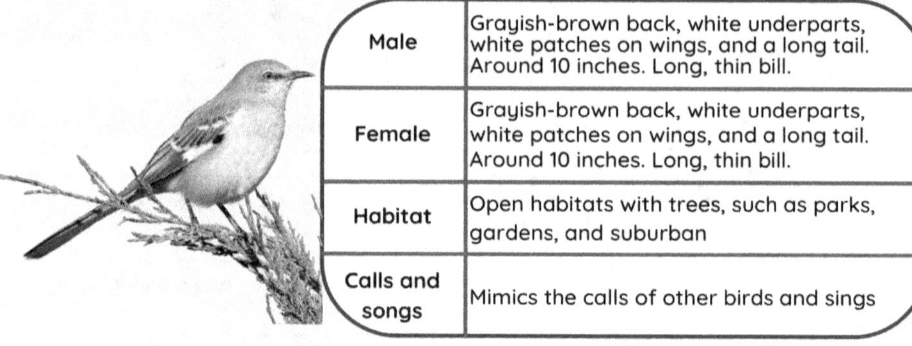

Male	Grayish-brown back, white underparts, white patches on wings, and a long tail. Around 10 inches. Long, thin bill.
Female	Grayish-brown back, white underparts, white patches on wings, and a long tail. Around 10 inches. Long, thin bill.
Habitat	Open habitats with trees, such as parks, gardens, and suburban
Calls and songs	Mimics the calls of other birds and sings

Yellow-rumped Warbler

Male	Blue-gray back, yellow throat, breast, and sides, and white belly. Around 5 inches. Yellow rump patch and streaked flanks.
Female	Gray-brown back, yellow throat, breast, and sides, and white belly. Around 5 inches. Yellow rump patch and streaked flanks.
Habitat	Coniferous forests, mixed forests, and suburban areas
Calls and songs	Sings a musical trill and a series of high-pitched notes.

Common Grackle

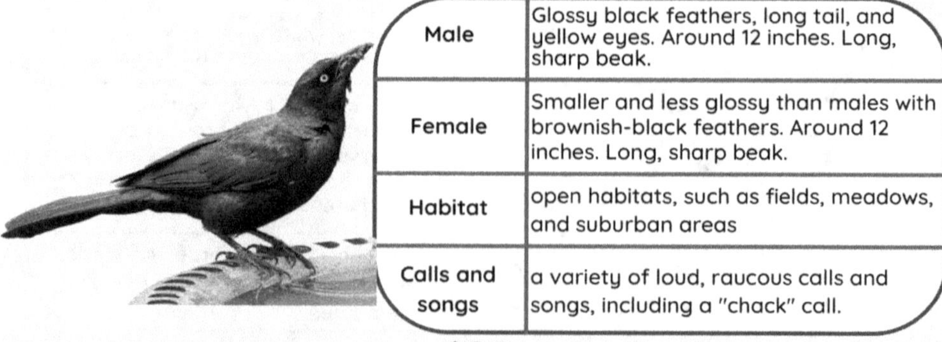

Male	Glossy black feathers, long tail, and yellow eyes. Around 12 inches. Long, sharp beak.
Female	Smaller and less glossy than males with brownish-black feathers. Around 12 inches. Long, sharp beak.
Habitat	open habitats, such as fields, meadows, and suburban areas
Calls and songs	a variety of loud, raucous calls and songs, including a "chack" call.

Male	Dark gray back, wings, and tail. Light gray underside with a black cap and bib. Around 4 inches.
Female	Similar to male but with a smaller black cap. Around 4 inches.
Habitat	Deciduous and mixed forests, woodlands, parks, and suburban areas
Calls and songs	a clear "chick-a-dee-dee-dee" call and a high-pitched trill.

Male	Dark gray overall with a black cap and rusty undertail. Around 8 inches.
Female	Similar to male but with a smaller black cap and less rusty undertail. Around 8 inches.
Habitat	Thickets, shrubs, and forest edges
Calls and songs	a wide range of songs and calls, including a musical "mew" and a cat-like "mrahh".

Male	Striped head with a white throat and yellow patch above the eye. Brown back and wings. Around 6.5 inches.
Female	Similar to male but with a duller head pattern. Around 6.5 inches.
Habitat	Brushy areas, forests, and suburban gardens
Calls and songs	Sings a clear, whistled "Oh sweet Canada Canada Canada" or "Old Sam Peabody Peabody Peabody" song, and has a variety of other calls.

Indigo Bunting

Male	Bright blue with black wings and tail
Female	Brownish-gray with a faint blue tinge
Habitat	Fields and open woodlands
Calls and songs	a sweet and cheerful song that sounds like "fire, fire, where, where, here, here, see it, see it".

Chipping Sparrow

Male	Rusty cap and back, gray face and underparts, black line through the eye. Around 5.5 inches.
Female	Similar to male but with a duller cap and less distinct eye line. Around 5.5 inches.
Habitat	open woods, parks, and gardens
Calls and songs	Sings a sweet, trilling song that sounds like "chip-chip-chipper-ee" or "chippewee", and has a high-pitched "tsip" call.

Eastern Bluebird

Male	Bright blue back, wings, and tail, rust-colored throat and breast, white belly. Around 7 inches.
Female	Grayish-blue back, wings, and tail, duller rust-colored throat and breast, white belly. Around 7 inches.
Habitat	open fields, meadows, and forest edges
Calls and songs	Sings a soft, warbling song that sounds like "chur-lee, chur-loo, chur-lie", and has a quiet, high-pitched "tew" call.

Brown-headed Cowbird

Male	Glossy black body and brown head. Around 7.5 inches.
Female	Gray-brown body and head. Around 7 inches.
Habitat	open grasslands, pastures, and agricultural areas
Calls and songs	Male makes a gurgling song and a buzzy "klink" call. Female makes a high-pitched "chit" or "chew" call.

Rock Pigeon

Male	Gray body with iridescent feathers on the neck, green and purple on the neck, and two black bands on the tail. Around 11 inches.
Female	Similar to male but less iridescence on the neck. Around 11 inches.
Habitat	cities and towns across the world.
Calls and songs	Makes a series of low-pitched coos that sound like "coo-coo-coo" or "coo-roo-coo-coo".

Common Yellowthroat

Male	Olive-green back and wings, yellow throat and breast with a black mask. Around 4.5 inches.
Female	Similar to male but with a duller mask and less distinct yellow throat and breast. Around 4.5 inches.
Habitat	Wetlands, marshes, and shrubby areas
Calls and songs	Sings a series of "wichity-wichity-wichity" notes followed by a "tichu-tichu-tichu" trill, and has a high-pitched "tik" call.

Eastern Phoebe

Male	Gray-brown back and wings, pale yellowish-white underparts, black bill. Around 6 inches.
Female	Similar to male but with a duller head and breast. Around 6 inches.
Habitat	near water such as streams, ponds, and swamps
Calls and songs	Repeats its name "phoebe" or "fee-bee" in a clear, whistled tone, and has a sharp "peep" call.

Ruby-crowned Kinglet

Male	Olive-green back and wings, white belly, and a red crown patch (which is not always visible). Around 4 inches.
Female	Similar to male but with a duller crown patch. Around 4 inches.
Habitat	coniferous forests and mixed woodlands
Calls and songs	Makes a high-pitched, warbling song that sounds like "tsee-tsee-tsee-tsee-tsee-tsee-tsu-tsu-tsu" and has a high-pitched "tsee" call.

Hairy Woodpecker

Male	Size: 9-10 inches Color: Black and white Bill is long, straight, and chisel-like.
Female	Same as male
Habitat	Woodlands with mature trees or forest edges.
Calls and songs	High, clear whistles of "peek" or "pik" sound, sometimes in a long string. A rapid drumming that sounds like a jackhammer is also heard during courtship or territorial disputes.

Cedar Waxwing

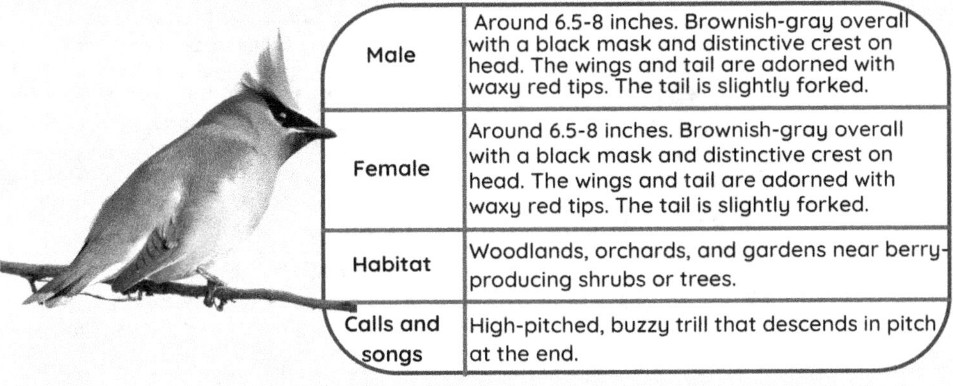

Male	Around 6.5-8 inches. Brownish-gray overall with a black mask and distinctive crest on head. The wings and tail are adorned with waxy red tips. The tail is slightly forked.
Female	Around 6.5-8 inches. Brownish-gray overall with a black mask and distinctive crest on head. The wings and tail are adorned with waxy red tips. The tail is slightly forked.
Habitat	Woodlands, orchards, and gardens near berry-producing shrubs or trees.
Calls and songs	High-pitched, buzzy trill that descends in pitch at the end.

House Wren

Male	Around 4.5 inches. Brown upperparts with a buff-colored belly. Short, curved bill.
Female	Around 4.5 inches. Brown upperparts with a buff-colored belly. Short, curved bill.
Habitat	Thick vegetation along streams, forest edges, or brushy areas.
Calls and songs	Loud, bubbly trills and chattering songs that can be repeated rapidly.

White-crowned Sparrow

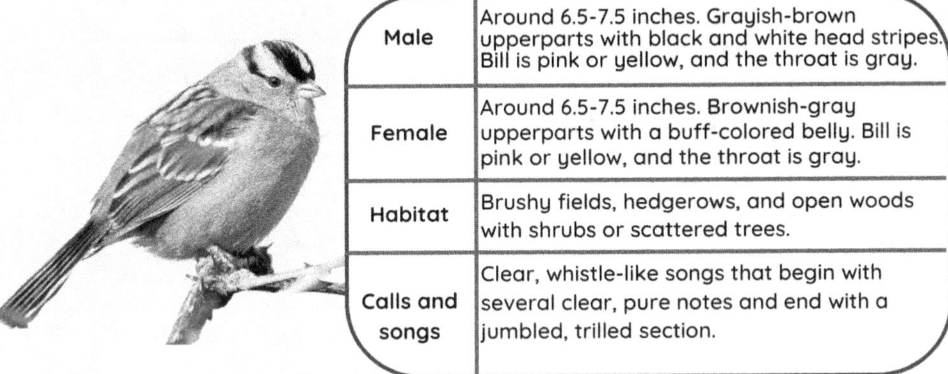

Male	Around 6.5-7.5 inches. Grayish-brown upperparts with black and white head stripes. Bill is pink or yellow, and the throat is gray.
Female	Around 6.5-7.5 inches. Brownish-gray upperparts with a buff-colored belly. Bill is pink or yellow, and the throat is gray.
Habitat	Brushy fields, hedgerows, and open woods with shrubs or scattered trees.
Calls and songs	Clear, whistle-like songs that begin with several clear, pure notes and end with a jumbled, trilled section.

Eastern Towhee

Male	Around 7-8 inches. Black upper parts with rusty sides and a white belly. Red eyes.
Female	Around 7-8 inches. Brownish-gray upper parts with a buff-colored belly. Brown eyes.
Habitat	Brushy areas and forest edges with dense undergrowth.
Calls and songs	The song is a cheerful "drink your tea!" with the first note higher than the other two. The call is a short, metallic "chink" or "tink" sound.

Yellow Warbler

Male	Bright yellow with red streaks on breast, thin beak
Female	Dull yellow with brownish streaks, thin beak
Habitat	Breeds in deciduous forests, winters in tropical areas
Calls and songs	High-pitched, sweet song that sounds like "sweet sweet sweet, I'm so sweet"

Pileated Woodpecker

Male	Black with a red crest on head, long chisel-like beak
Female	Similar to male, but lacks red crest and has a black forehead
Habitat	mature forests
Calls and songs	Loud, high-pitched "wuk wuk wuk" call, often heard drumming on trees to find food

Red-eyed Vireo

Male	Olive green with a white eyebrow and red eyes
Female	Similar to male, but slightly duller in color
Habitat	deciduous forests
Calls and songs	Monotonous song with a repeated phrase that sounds like "here I am, where are you?"

Anna's Hummingbird

Male	Shimmering green back, reddish-pink head and throat.
Female	Duller with a gray-green back and pale throat
Habitat	open woodlands, coastal scrub, gardens, and parks. Also urban areas, including suburban gardens and city parks.
Calls and songs	High-pitched, buzzy "chip" call and a loud metallic "cheeep" call; males perform aerial displays called "courtship dives"

Red-breasted Nuthatch

Male	Blue-gray back, rusty-orange breast and sides
Female	Similar to male, but with a paler head and breast
Habitat	Coniferous forests
Calls and songs	Nasal, tinny "yank yank" call that sounds like a toy trumpet; often heard descending trees headfirst while foraging for food

Spotted Towhee

Male	Black head, wings, and tail, rusty sides and back
Female	Brownish-gray head and back, rust-colored sides
Habitat	shrubby areas
Calls and songs	Loud, scratchy "chewink" call, often heard singing from a perch or foraging on the ground

Ruby-throated Hummingbird

Male	Bright green back and crown, iridescent red throat
Female	Duller with a pale throat
Habitat	deciduous forests, mixed forests, and forest edges. Also gardens, parks, and other areas with flowering plants.
Calls and songs	High-pitched "chirp" call and a high-pitched "zipping" sound made by the wings during flight; males perform aerial displays called "courtship dives"

Lesser Goldfinch

Male	Bright yellow underparts, black cap and wings
Female	Duller with a gray-green back and pale underparts
Habitat	Scrubby habitats
Calls and songs	Melodic, warbling song with a series of twittering notes that sound like "per-chik-o-ree" or "ti-di-di-di"

These pages are for you to write down your thoughts and experiences about the birds you saw. You can write about which bird was your favorite, what you liked about it, and any other thoughts or feelings you have about bird watching.

SUMMARY NOTES

SPREAD YOUR WINGS AND FLY TOWARD YOUR DREAMS

bird species word search
(page 103)

bird-watching word search
(page 107)

lovebird maze
(page 101)

bird tree maze
(page 109)

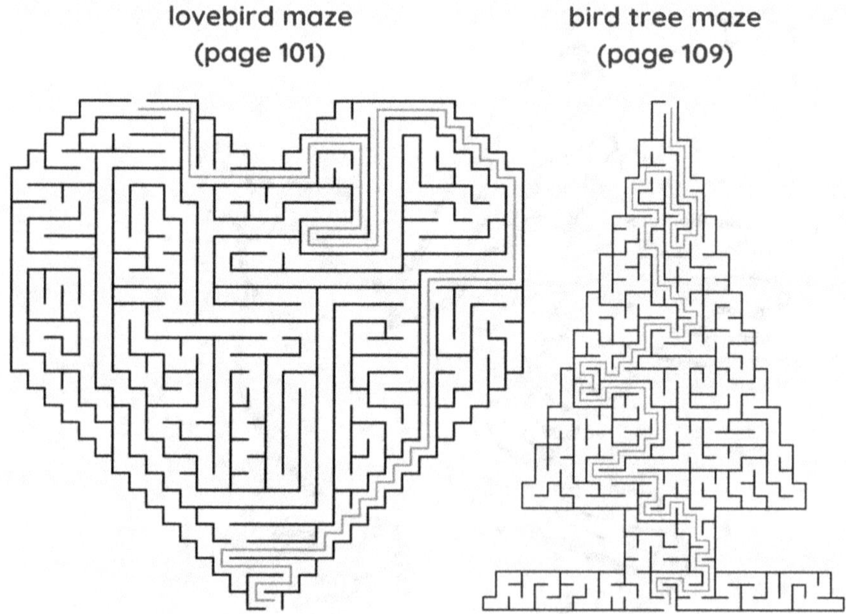

Meet the Author

Growing up in a low-means family, books became my best friends. I was a true bookworm, spending countless hours at the library after school, exploring magical worlds and sparking my imagination.

As I became a mother to four wonderful boys, I want to share my love of books with them. But with technology taking over, I realized it wasn't easy.

That's when I made it my mission to create fun and engaging books that would capture the hearts and minds of young readers. My goal is to inspire a love of reading, encouraging kids to put down their tablets and pick up a book.

Whether you're a parent looking for quality time with your little ones or a child eager for a new adventure, I invite you to join me on this journey to keep the magic of books alive for years to come.

Yours,
Iris Moran